Making Tootsie

Making Tootsie

A Film Study With
Dustin Hoffman and Sydney Pollack

by Susan Dworkin

Newmarket Press   New York

First Edition
1   2   3   4   5   6   7   8   9   0

The publisher wishes to acknowledge the cooperation of Columbia Pictures in the publication of this book.

All material quoted from the screenplay Tootsie *reprinted with permission of Columbia Pictures Industries, Inc.*
Text and cover photographs taken during the shoot of Tootsie *by Brian Hamill.*
Cover photograph of Dustin Hoffman as Dorothy by Greg Gorman.
Cover design by Mike Stromberg
Book design by Levavi & Lavavi
Library of Congress Catalog Card Number: 83-2355

ISBN 0-937858-19-6
Manufactured in the United States of America

Acknowledgments

The author wishes to acknowledge with gratitude the help of her editor, Bette Alexander, and her publisher, Esther Margolis, in preparing the manuscript, as well as Lucy O'Brien and Grace Kubrin who typed and retyped it. Thanks are due to all those from the company and crew of Tootsie who shared their thoughts and gave their time to this book. And a special debt is owed to Rocky Lang for his generous assistance and to Ann Guerin, for her support and wise counsel.

I THE WHOLE TRICK WITH
Tootsie was to get Dustin Hoffman to look like a *real* woman, so
that the characters around him in the movie could believe he was a
woman and not appear ridiculous for doing so. In Hoffman's contract, there was actually a clause stipulating that reality had to be
achieved before shooting could begin.

This meant that *Tootsie* differed in comic intent from *Some Like
It Hot*, the Billy Wilder classic in which Marilyn Monroe and Joe E.
Brown had so engagingly been duped by two hairy "girls," Tony
Curtis and Jack Lemmon. Hoffman would not be hairy. His muscles
wouldn't show. Nor would his Adam's apple. A vibrant, wiry man
with burning brown eyes and the nervous energy of a prizefighter, he
intended to bury himself in *Tootsie*, to disappear into her disguises.

Tootsie joined a cluster of gender-switch comedies that included
La Cage Aux Folles I and *II*, *Victor, Victoria* and *The World Ac-
cording to Garp*, which featured John Lithgow's transsexual Roberta.
(When *Tootsie* began shooting in April 1982, Barbra Streisand's
Yentl was still in preparation.)

1

The theatre, which always has a way of being first, had begun the recent trend two years earlier with Caryl Churchill's *Cloud 9*, directed by Tommy Tune. In this send-up of both sexism and imperialism, men played Victorian matrons, women played Victorian boys, and white men played black men as well as little girls in contemporary London. In *The Singular Life of Albert Nobbs*, by Simone Benmussa, Glenn Close played a woman who spent her entire adult life impersonating an Irish waiter. This play was on at the Manhattan Theatre Club uptown while *Tootsie* was shooting in New York, and Hoffman questioned any colleague who went to see it about the details of Close's highly realistic performance.

Although filming lasted 98 days, Hoffman, now 45, invested almost four years of his life in *Tootsie*, a Columbia Pictures comedy about a down-and-out actor who gets his big break by impersonating an actress. Four years is a long time for a star performer to voluntarily absent himself from the screen—all the more so since Hoffman's last performance in *Kramer vs. Kramer* had won him an Academy Award and a secure reputation as one of our finest actors.

His willingness to devote so much time to *Tootsie* stemmed from his interest in taking that range of journeys which justifies the madness and hassle of the acting profession. In *The Graduate*, his hilarious portrayal of a young man seduced by an older woman won him an Oscar nomination. He was nominated again when he played the seedy derelict Ratzo Rizzo in *Midnight Cowboy* and again for his portrayal of the doomed comedian Lenny Bruce in *Lenny*. Range was overwhelmingly artistic. Hoffman was not looking for the truth in *All the President's Men*, an indefatigable journalist; in *Straw Dogs*, an avenging intellectual. His desire to play a woman in *Tootsie* may have appeared political in the context of the times, but in fact, it was overwhelmingly artistic. Hoffman was not looking for the truth about women. He was looking for the woman in himself.

The man who finally directed and produced *Tootsie* was Sydney Pollack. Pollack had not worked with Hoffman before, nor had he ever directed an out-and-out bare-faced comedy. His forte was grown-up, rational romance. His hallmark was melancholy. There were deep creases in his face. A tall, 48 year old man with curly, greying hair and large, expressive hands, he was known in the trade as a "lion-tamer," because of his excellent track record in handling big stars like Barbra Streisand (*The Way We Were*), Robert Redford (*This Property is Condemned, Jeremiah Johnson, The Way We Were, Three Days of the Condor, The Electric Horseman*), Paul Newman and Sally Field (*Absence of Malice*), Faye Dunaway (*Three Days of the Condor*), Jane Fonda (*They Shoot Horses, Don't They?, The Electric Horseman*) and Al Pacino (*Bobby Deerfield*). He was trusted by Columbia Pictures because of his extraordinary success at bringing in *Absence of Malice* $1 million *under* budget (a Hollywood rarity) and because six of his eight last movies had made money.

From the earliest make-up tests in Los Angeles, all through the arduous shoot in the dead heat of a New York summer, Sydney Pollack and Dustin Hoffman never gave *Tootsie* a rest. They never gave each other a rest. To keep themselves going, they ate like lab animals. Sydney stopped smoking. He went on the Pritikin diet and took a substantial segment of the company with him. Long after many others had reverted to red meat, he was still incessantly chewing celery and gum and peaches.

Dustin got Vitamin B12 shots. He kept a jump rope on hand at the set and between takes he would skip at it in short bursts of awesome speed.

Sydney hired a U.S.C. coach to teach him aerobic swimming because when he ran, his back went out.

Dustin, who is devoted to the chicken fat saturated fare at Sammy's Rumanian downtown, dutifully ate lentil soup.

They were so concentrated on *Tootsie*, with that bunker mentality peculiar to movie sets, that they could pay little attention to the war in Lebanon which occupied the summer of their fellow-Jews everywhere.

They listened so hard to each other, during long arguments about text and subtext, that after a while, they began to talk alike.

"The truth of the matter is . . ." they'd say.

"In other words . . ." they'd re-explain.

The intercoastal rumor mills processed their conflicts with delighted zeal all the way through the shoot. Their fights made the trade papers. Their reconciliations did not. Even people only remotely associated with the film had to constantly reassert that the collaboration had not dissolved.

3

No, Sydney and Dustin had not come to blows.

No, Dustin's hand injury had not kept him off the set for a week. More like two hours.

No, the budget wasn't already up to $32 million.

"We've made Hollywood the happiest bunch of people in the world by our problems here," Sydney said. "Because everybody's had something to talk about at a cocktail party. Their eyes light up at the next disaster."

The affection for "disaster stories" was caused by the hot combination of jealousy and guilt that characterized Hollywood. Jealousy because you thought you were just as good as Dustin Hoffman or Sydney Pollack, but they had the picture and its millions and oh, it would be so wonderful to see them fall on their faces. Guilt because many individuals in the movie business were overpaid, and out there in America, where more and more people were wandering jobless, class anger at the film industry in general was always a possibility.

If the industry thrived on disaster stories, it was not really to hurt people like Sydney and Dustin, but to keep alive the idea that the risks were so high, the pressures so unbearable, the fall from grace so imminent and terrifying, that the money so many were making might actually be justified.

But the worst of the pressure did not come from anticipation of disaster; both men had lived through that. It was the expectation of *success* that worried them; the idea—firmly held by studio executives and Wall Street analysts—that if Dustin Hoffman was going to dress up like a girl in a comedy written by Larry (*M*A*S*H*) Gelbart and Murray Schisgal and produced and directed by Sydney Pollack for release in December of 1982, it was going to be a very merry Christmas for all.

And although it is rare that two men so unsuited by taste, temperament and inner music should collaborate on a major motion picture . . .

And although the tension between them was sometimes so powerful that the set seemed to be on the verge of emotional meltdown . . .

They did do quite a job together on *Tootsie*, which would strike millions of Americans as the funniest movie in years.

4

. . .

The hero of *Tootsie* is Michael Dorsey, an out-of-work actor pushing forty and getting nowhere in the New York theatre. Despite the fact that he is renowned for his talent, he loses jobs because he is considered temperamental and difficult; he works as a waiter, teaches acting, auditions constantly but with little success, and shares a loft in Chelsea with Jeff, a flaky playwright (Bill Murray).

Michael's fondest hope is to raise enough money to produce Jeff's play so he can perform in it with his friend and longtime acting student, Sandy (Teri Garr). Michael coaches Sandy for an audition for the role of the tough-cookie hospital administrator on a popular television soap opera. But Sandy doesn't even get a chance to read. She's rejected because she's not a tough cookie. Michael finds out that an ex-friend who has less talent than he has landed a big role in *The Iceman Cometh* on Broadway and, furious, he storms into his agent's office demanding to know why he wasn't sent to audition. The agent (Sydney Pollack), a slick show business power with all lines open to "the Coast," declares that Michael is so difficult, no one will hire him.

To show up his unsympathetic agent, Michael puts on make-up, a wig and women's clothes, tries out for the role that Sandy didn't get to read for, and becomes in a flash the hospital administrator of *Southwest General*, Ms. Emily Kimberly.

Assuming the name of Dorothy Michaels, Michael settles in at the soap, where he meets a beautiful co-worker, Julie (Jessica Lange). A close friendship develops between Dorothy and Julie.

This is a new experience for Michael. Being trusted by a woman. Having innocent fun with a woman. Being *friends* with a woman. He even gets to babysit for Amy, Julie's beautiful blonde baby. Julie invites Dorothy up to her father's farm for the weekend. They have a wonderful time. They talk wallpaper and milk cows. Julie's widowed father, Les (Charles Durning), promptly falls in love with Dorothy.

And Dorothy, who is—after all—Michael Dorsey, falls in love with Julie.

In his other life as a man, Michael seduces Sandy one night, kind of by mistake. When he subsequently neglects her, she concludes he's gay. When Michael, in the guise of Dorothy, allows some of his passion for Julie to surface, she concludes that Dorothy's a lesbian. Les, on the other hand, proposes marriage.

What started out as contemporary situation comedy has turned into classical farce. Quick changes. Multiple identities. Wild confusion. Michael finally confesses during a live broadcast of the soap that in fact he is not Emily Kimberly, that he is not even female, and strips off his wig and his eyelashes to prove it.

Richer for his experience—both figuratively, since he has learned how it feels to be a woman—and literally, since he now has enough money to produce Jeff's play, Michael manages to secure both the forgiveness and friendship of Les and the forgiveness and love of Julie. "I was a better man with you, as a woman," he tells her, "than I ever was with a woman as a man . . . I've just got to do it without the dress."

This happy ending took place after innumerable takes on the recently revitalized section of West 42nd Street known as Theatre Row. It was one of the shoot's many 90 degree days. Dustin was in pain from an injured hand, which had been caught under a door in a freak accident; between takes, he slipped his arm into a sling. David McGiffert, the first assistant director, was deploying *Tootsie* staff to manage the crowds of New Yorkers who gaped and gawked and had to be held in friendly check lest they wander into the movie. Owen Roizman, the laid-back, athletic director of photography, scowled at the passing clouds, waiting for them to release the sun so he could finish filming the outdoor scene. The movie was costing $80,000 a day. If you figure twelve hours in the working day, that's $110 a minute. Waiting was expensive.

Sydney Pollack, beset by unavoidable delays, beset by script problems and wounded star problems, got so hot and sweaty that he hung out his shirt to dry.

And Mikhail Baryshnikov, the father of Jessica Lange's *real* beautiful blonde baby, sat in Jessica's chair and watched and smiled the calm smile of the non-involved.

.   .   .

6

Although the storyline of *Tootsie* was simple and straightforward enough, the script history of the film was anything but. "You can't write a party," Sydney Pollack said when he was trying to stage one in the loft on 18th Street where Michael and Jeff lived. Too many people. Too much action. Too much background. That was just what writing *Tootsie* was like. Such a big party, so many people, so much action, that it's a miracle it got written at all.

The script started roughly with Charles Evans, a busy, business-like man with a beautiful office. Modern sculpture reflected in a wall of mirrors. A mottled green marble floor. An incidental curved wall of opaque glass bricks (like the one in *It's My Turn*).

Evans, the executive producer of *Tootsie*, was the man who owned the script when it first came to the attention of Dustin Hoffman. It had come to Evans' attention in 1978 through Buddy Hackett, the comedian, who wanted to play the role of the agent. The script Hackett showed his friend Charles Evans was called *Would I Lie to You?*, and it had been written by Don McGuire.

"When Buddy Hackett sent me the script," Evans recalled, "I called him and said: 'This is terrific.' I didn't know Henry Plitt (of the Plitt Theatre Chain) who owned the McGuire script. But I called Henry Plitt. Told him I liked the script. Would he like to sell it? And he said yes. Two days later I went to California. Went right to Henry's office. Told him I'd like to buy it. So we started talking price. Plitt owned the script with two other people. He needed their permisson. And McGuire had a piece of whatever would happen to the picture if it got made. So when I bought the property, Plitt had to negotiate with his other partners, and I had to negotiate with McGuire and make a different deal with him."

Evans realized he was coming into a property that had switched owners and been turned down a few times. But he characterizes himself as a man unimpressed by prior opinions. "I thought it was funny. And no one could tell me it wasn't. In talking with McGuire, I knew that he'd gone about as far as he could with it. I knew it needed a rewrite desperately. I knew I had to pay for a new script. I met a lot of comedy writers. Met Bob Kaufman. His ideas coincided with mine."

Bob Kaufman was retained by Evans in 1979. According to Kaufman, his rewrite of *Would I Lie to You?* was to be "a $4½ million extended sitcom." George Hamilton, who had starred in another Kaufman comedy, *Love at First Bite*, was to play the lead. He and Kaufman were to be executive producers. Charles Evans was to be producer.

During the period that Kaufman was on retainer to Evans, Evans showed the property to a friend, director Dick Richards. Richards was interested.

"I put Kaufman in a hotel room," Dick Richards recalled, "and I harassed him into writing and we cracked each other up." For fifteen days, Kaufman and Richards, joined by Evans, worked in the Sherry Netherland in New York—"with Richards giving me advice," Kaufman chortled. "Like: 'Fill up the pages faster!'"

Finally they had a new script. It was about an out-of-work actor who gets a job playing a nurse on a soap opera.

"It was very funny," Evans said. "Definitely needed a rewrite."

"At that time I had such confidence in the project that I wasn't sure I wanted George (Hamilton) to play the lead. But the deal that I had with Kaufman locked up Kaufman and Hamilton together . . . I had nothing against George. George is a good actor. But at this point, I saw somebody different. I thought about Chevy Chase; Elliott Gould, who would have liked to have done it, but he'd be too funny-looking a nurse; George Segal . . . but then I thought he was too old. And before I talked to anyone else I wanted to finish the script."

At this time, Charles Evans showed the script to his brother, Bob, an experienced Hollywood hand who had produced such films as *Black Sunday* and *Marathon Man*. Bob was not crazy about the script. He thought it had no middle and that the main character needed a background; a childhood; roots. Charles Evans said he did not necessarily agree. However, "I was persuaded to go along with my brother. Richards was also. . . . But in my case, there was a good reason to take that point of view because I would be free to use whomever I wanted."

So Bob Kaufman departed the picture. George Hamilton went off to play a wacky bandit king in *Zorro, the Gay Blade*, and Dick Richards was encouraged by Charles Evans to show the script to Dustin Hoffman, with whom Richards had formed a company for the development of properties. Hoffman read the script on an airplane and liked it. Dustin and playwright Murray Schisgal had been talking for some time about the possibility that Dustin might play a female character; they shared the notion that inside every man, there lurked the woman he might have been; affectionately, they called this abstract female "Shirley." They had begun working on a script about a male tennis player who passes as a woman and gets all the way to Wimbledon before he is finally beaten by a thirteen-year-old girl. So Dustin was already geared up for a gender-switch film, and the Evans property struck a responsive chord. Murray Schisgal now became *Tootsie*'s third writer. Shortly after Schisgal came on board, Dick Richards—who would ultimately be listed as co-producer with Sydney Pollack—departed the picture.

Primarily a playwright, Murray Schisgal was the author of *Luv, The Typist and The Tiger* and *Jimmy Shine,* in which Dustin had starred. His newest play, *Twice Around the Park* starring Eli Wallach and Anne Jackson, would open on Broadway soon after the *Tootsie* shoot came to an end in August 1982.

While the personnel of *Tootsie* continued shifting, Charles Evans, meanwhile, had had to buy back the property "once or twice" from Henry Plitt, to whom it reverted if not produced within a certain time.

"I started working with Dustin," Evans said, "started spending quite a bit of time at his house. I hadn't made my deal with Columbia yet. I made my deal with Columbia only when Dustin said: Yes, I definitely want to do this.

"The only way Dustin would make a commitment would be if he gained complete control. He wanted to be the producer or the pre-senter. He wanted to be in control of the script and everything else. I didn't care. I was happy having Dustin Hoffman do my first movie. I thought it was quite a coup for me, my very first film. So I made a deal with Columbia where I moved myself back to executive producer."

It was Dustin who named the property *Tootsie*. The title, he said, came from his mother. "She used to throw me up in the air and say 'How's my Tootsie Wootsie?!' The only thing she wanted, more than anything else, was to see this movie happen." (Dustin's mother died the year before *Tootsie* was completed.)

Tootsie needed a director, and Dustin wanted Hal Ashby. As Dustin related it, he had wanted Ashby to work with him on *Straight Time,* but Ashby was then cutting *Bound for Glory.* Ashby

9

had wanted Hoffman to be in *Coming Home,* but Dustin was then involved with *Straight Time.*

"So when this project came along," Dustin explained, "I got Hal Ashby. But Hal was still cutting what he had done with Jon Voight (*Looking To Get Out,* which opened in October '82). And since he couldn't get out of the cutting end, at a certain point Columbia said to me: 'You cannot do this picture with Hal Ashby.' And they suggested Sydney Pollack."

Columbia also convinced Dustin that he should not continue doing the picture with Murray Schisgal, and suggested Larry Gelbart, creator of the television version of *M*A*S*H,* as a replacement. Gelbart then became *Tootsie's* fourth writer.

In November 1981, Sydney Pollack took over as director and producer, with a deal that gave him control of casting, the script, and the final cut.

"Larry Gelbart and Sydney and I met for like nine days (at Sydney's beach house)," Dustin says. "And a lot of the things Sydney said I liked and a lot of things I disagreed with. I used to go home and talk to my wife about it. I was in that bind. I used to say to her, I don't know what to do. It's not a personal thing, it's a gut thing, I mean when you get into the ring . . . I'm a certain kind of fighter. So I work best when I work with another guy who's fighting with me in a certain kind of way. If you're right-handed and you know you throw a combination bump bump banh and you get in with a southpaw, well a southpaw makes anybody look bad . . . everything is combinations . . . so you wonder whether this director and you are the right *fighting* combination. And I feel that all good films have to fight. In other words, it's a *good fight* . . . You do three minutes. When the round's over, you hope you went at it, you give each other a tap, you go sit down, you rest, look at each other from across the ring, you know, you get the cut man on you, and then you go in and fight again. It's like any good marriage, I think. You're fighting for territory. And you want it to be 50-50."

This is an idealized version of collaboration, the fond hope of an actor struggling for control over his own work in a medium where "final cut"—the last say on the last edited version—is the ultimate venue of control. Even as Dustin Hoffman described his vision of "a good fight" he knew full well that "50-50" would be hard to come by, that Pollack had "final cut," that whatever artistic struggles passed between them might be resolved by Sydney alone with Sydney's editors in Sydney's cutting room. It haunted Hoffman, that vision of *Tootsie*'s last days. It never left his mind. And he spared no effort to guarantee that what he loved in the movie would somehow survive.

Sydney for all his contracted authority felt that he couldn't just use it like a sledge hammer. Dustin was the project's throbbing heart. His enthusiasm was essential. His agreement was essential. "At one time this was Dustin's picture," Sydney told *Variety*. "He fathered it along and he had to live with the idea that I was directing it." Sydney knew that Dustin couldn't do what he didn't love. He was an actor, not a clause in a contract. So when Dustin wanted to talk script, or talk casting, Sydney was available.

Whatever disagreements Dustin and Sydney may have had over casting stemmed from differences in style, not substance. When Dustin had had control of the film, he had extended *feelers* on casting but he had not been able to implement his decisions because there was no director, no budget; and in any case Dustin is, stylistically, not a finalizer. He ponders; he changes his mind; he tries this, tries that; he casts like an actor.

When Sydney came on board, he knew exactly whom he wanted. "All these people are first choices," he says proudly of his cast. He knew how much he wanted to pay; he knew what quality he wanted in each role. Stylistically, he is preemptive, ready to discuss matters as long as they wind up more or less where he desired them to be in the first place. He casts like a director.

What made casting *Tootsie* a relatively smooth process was the fact that both men essentially agreed on what good acting was and who good actors were. They had both been trained in the Method system, pioneered by people like Harold Clurman, Sanford Meisner, Lee Strasberg, Stella Adler, and Elia Kazan, all of whom hailed from the Group Theatre of the '30's.

Sydney's mentor was Sanford Meisner, who founded the Neighborhood Playhouse. When Pollack set out from South Bend, Indiana to be an actor right after his high school graduation in 1952 (and over his father's objections), he came to New York and studied there. Eventually Pollack became Meisner's assistant, then heir apparent. When Dustin Hoffman quit college to become an actor, he initially took classes at the Pasadena Playhouse. But then he too headed for New York, in 1958, and one of the places he studied was the Actors' Studio, founded by Lee Strasberg.

Such teachers as Meisner and Strasberg had made the ideas of Konstantin Stanislavsky the dominant force in American drama coaching. They taught actors to achieve emotional reality by finding the truth of the role in themselves. Sometimes this involved the use of *affective* or *sense memory*. The actor recalled how he felt at a moment in his past similar to the moment in the play, and let his memory affect the performance. If the scene says you have to be in love with this quirky actress you'd prefer not to take a bus with, then you must summon how you felt when you were falling in love with your *real* lover: how she frightened you; how she made you laugh; how she turned you on; all of it; until you could look at the quirky actress and feel that way again. This is very hard to do. Very hard. When it is done well, even the untrained eye sees truth and finds delight. Name a good American actor and a memorable performance in the United States and chances are the Method of the Group Theatre teachers is somewhere in the background.

Although it would be wrong to trace Sydney and Dustin back to their teachers in any strict way, some major themes have survived.

Lee Strasberg, wrote Harold Clurman, "was a fanatic on the subject of true emotion," and so is Dustin; a fanatic.

Sanford Meisner had co-directed with Clifford Odets the first production of Odets' *Waiting for Lefty* which had made the Group famous for more than just theory. His students recalled that Meisner had a sign in his studio that said: good acting was true behavior in imaginary circumstances. Sydney, when he gave up acting to become a director, remained committed to the creation of pragmatically constructed imaginary circumstances that would serve as dramatic bedrock for true behavior.

By the time *Tootsie* was in production, Clurman and Strasberg had died, Meisner was ill and the ethos of the Group and the Method had worn down under fifty years of reinterpretation and more or less constant misuse. The British, who didn't need to re-

12

locate personally in the atmosphere of a role just to play the role, still seemed to be able to play their roles with emotional truth. (Brian Clark, the English author of *Whose Life Is It Anyway?* was appalled by the way some American actors felt compelled to haunt hospitals for weeks just to play nurses.) Many younger American theatre writers had grown cynical when not despairing at the way so many actors displayed contempt for the text while supposedly searching for "true behavior."

But the most unrelenting pressure on pure theatrical ideals came from the erosion of the medium in which they had grown. Most American actors in 1982 weren't judged by their performances on legitimate stages. They were judged by their work on television and in the movies. And it is a vastly different thing to perform an undeniable script before a living audience that is breathing energy at you across the footlights than to perform before the glass and steel nose of the indifferent camera, using a script that can be changed summarily without recourse to its writers, in scenes that are shot in a sequence determined by location rather than narrative continuity.

Dustin had been part of this world of flickering screens since his first starring role in *The Graduate* in 1967. Sydney had joined it even earlier. But Dustin and Sydney still evaluated the craft of acting with a vital "sense memory" of what it was like when they were in the theatre, before the intervention of cameras and editing machines. When it came to casting, they came from the same culture.

There was no argument about casting Charles Durning, a seasoned actor in all media, as Les, the farmer who falls in love with his daughter's soap opera colleague, Dorothy Michaels. Durning had been cast in *Tootsie* when the film was still set to be directed by Hal Ashby. It was left up to Sydney to keep him or not, and Sydney kept him. There was no argument either about Teri Garr, who "came from the boards like I did," Dustin said, and whom Sydney had admired for her comedic innocence ever since he had seen her in *Young Frankenstein*.

Dustin was less familiar with the work of George Gaynes, whom Sydney wanted for the role of John Van Horn, Dorothy Michaels' elegant but horny soap co-star. George, who had appeared in *The Way We Were*, characterized himself as a member of "the semifloating repertory company" which people like Sydney and casting director Lynn Stalmaster often used to fill choice character roles.

And Dustin, who would have to be kissed by George and even survive an attempted rape by George, seemed happy with the choice. For the role of Rita, the hard-boiled soap opera producer, Dustin's choice was his close friend Polly Holliday (TV's "Flo"). Sydney, however, preferred to cast the soap opera characters from the ranks of the real article, and decided on Doris Belack, a seasoned soap star who had graduated to nighttime TV with *Baker's Dozen*.

Dustin got his choice for Jeff, the flaky playwright, when the role went to Bill Murray. Murray had come to national attention on television's *Saturday Night Live*, where "the actors," as Sydney said, "directed the actors," and the comedy was highly improvisational. He continued improvising on *Tootsie*. You never knew what was going to come out of his mouth. "Bill is every Jewish director's nightmare," Dustin laughed one evening at dailies, "because he has no guilt."

For Julie, the gentle soap opera actress with whom Michael Dorsey falls in love, Sydney wanted Jessica Lange. Dustin in the pre-Pollack days had interviewed well over 100 actresses for this role, and one or two were quite sure they had it in the bag. But Sydney favored Jessica, and his reasons were far from anything imagined by the Group Theatre.

"The role (of Julie) required that you understand immediately why he's in love with her," Sydney said. "And that has nothing to do with logic. It has to do with *quality on film*. There was never a question why anyone was in love with Marilyn Monroe. She walked in a room and the guy would go . . . (Sydney looked the way he would look if he had just seen Marilyn Monroe for the first time) . . . and you shot a close up of him and the audience said, 'That's it, they're in love.' Well, it saves you pages. And pages. And pages. Jessica Lange had it for me, in *King Kong* of all things. I made a mental note: *There's* a movie star.

"Most of the fine American actresses were too old for this part. And anyway, the movie couldn't take another $4 million dollar performer. (Dustin was being paid $4½ million.) I had to have someone affordable, who brought a little panache, to play this part . . . but almost more important, who could speak the *shorthand* to the audience. Because the love story in this picture is not in the scenes. She doesn't even get to know he's a man until almost the last scene in the movie! The love story is in the *longing* that Michael feels."

There was little argument that Jessica Lange could inspire longing.

The Postman Always Rings Twice had established the sloe-eyed blonde as a seething sensual power. Her graceful angel of death in *All That Jazz* had instilled her film persona with an exciting touch of evil. *Frances,* which opened almost simultaneously with *Tootsie,* established her as a powerful dramatic actress, in the running for an Oscar in 1983. *Tootsie* was to be Jessica's comedy. But it was "the longing," the sexual "shorthand" that ultimately made her irresistible in the casting discussions.

Casting hit its biggest snag over the role of George Fields, the theatrical agent whose lack of faith drives Michael Dorsey to put on a dress and become an actress.

Buddy Hackett had started *Tootsie* rolling so he could play this part. But Sydney Pollack wanted Dabney Coleman to play it. And Dustin Hoffman wanted Sydney Pollack to play it.

Dabney Coleman is an urbane, handsome man who seems to be picking up where George Sanders left off. After his nefarious evangelist in *Mary Hartman, Mary Hartman* and his sexist boss in *9 to 5,* he was well on his way to becoming the best loved male chauvinist in America. After being induced into acting by the late actor Zachary Scott, he studied his craft at the Neighborhood Playhouse, and became lifelong friends with his teacher Sydney Pollack. Dabney's most recent success in *On Golden Pond* had deepened Sydney's commitment to casting him.

But Dustin said he wanted Sydney Pollack to play his agent.

"He said I intimidated him!" Sydney laughed. "He said: 'Dabney is a peer. Dabney is not an authority figure. Dabney is not gonna scare me into putting on a dress!' "

Sydney said no, he didn't want to appear in a movie he was directing.

Dustin persisted—and Dustin can really persist.

"My own agent who's his agent called me up and started advising me to do it," Sydney said. "He had his lawyer pushing. He sent me *flowers!* With notes! 'PLEASE BE MY AGENT! LOVE, DOROTHY.' The truth of the matter is if I'm good in this picture, I have to give Dustin credit. Because he cast me."

The role of Ron, the charming, insensitive soap opera director, went to Dabney Coleman.

. . .

When it came to dealing with the script, the common bond of the Method helped little to bridge the gap between Pollack and Hoffman. They found it difficult to agree on what good writing was and who good writers were. Therefore, the script of *Tootsie* was never truly settled between them and remained a focus of debate throughout the shoot.

Larry Gelbart, the fourth *Tootsie* writer, made the film whole and viable, established its themes, fleshed out its characters, and replaced some of its early ribaldry with the ironic situation humor for which *M*A*S*H* had become famous. A seasoned comedy writer, Gelbart had come to Hollywood by way of *Caesar's Hour*, a successor to *The Show of Shows*, and had worked on Sid Caesar's team with Mel Brooks, Carl Reiner, Neil Simon and Woody Allen.

But Larry Gelbart also had his finger on the pulse of classic humor, the reliable elements of farce handed down from Shakespeare and Goldoni. With Burt Shevelove, Gelbart had reworked Plautus into *A Funny Thing Happened on the Way to the Forum*, which was funny enough to contain Zero Mostel as its star. Gelbart had picked up where Ben Jonson left off and had adapted *Volpone* into *Sly Fox* starring George C. Scott on Broadway.

His *Tootsie* smacked of Shakespeare's *Twelfth Night* and Goldoni's *Servant of Two Masters*, in which women dress up as men for perfectly good and innocent reasons and then can't admit they're in love with the men they're in love with and are fallen in love with by perfectly good and innocent women and are challenged to duels by men who think they're men. It's all very confusing, but it works.

What Sydney called the "Girl Talk Scene" in *Tootsie* was inspired, he said, by the way "ladies sit on sofas with their legs up under them, talking." A contemporary inspiration. But this "Girl Talk Scene," in which Dorothy and Julie discuss how hard it is to be "a woman in the 80s'" also seemed reminiscent of the "Man Talk" scene in *Twelfth Night*, in which Count Orsino discusses with his page Cesario how hard it is to be a man whose love is "hungry as the sea." Cesario, who is really Viola in disguise and just as much in love with Orsino as Michael-disguised-as-Dorothy is in love with Julie, has to stay cool and keep quiet.

16

When John Van Horn, the horny soap star, challenges Dorothy to a bout of "straight sex," it's funny the way it's funny when Sir Andrew Aguecheek challenges Viola to a duel in *Twelfth Night*. When Michael Dorsey races around from Julie's dinner to Sandy's dinner, trying to be a woman for one and a man for the other, it's funny the way it's funny when Truffaldino tries to serve two dinners simultaneously in *Servant of Two Masters*, one to a man and one to a woman disguised as a man. And you're laughing not because gender-switch is funny in America circa 1983 but because gender-switch has *always* been funny; it was laying them in the aisles in Venice circa 1783.

Gelbart worked on *Tootsie* for the better part of two years. He made his exit having essentially finished the script. He would share the credit with Murray Schisgal, after a Writers Guild arbitration. "In California," he was quoted in a *New York Times* interview, "they've got writers by the six-pack. If you're around long enough, there's no project that doesn't contain your work—rewritten."

Elaine May, author of *A New Leaf* and one of the film industry's most trusted comedy physicians, came in for three weeks to work with Sydney . . . who was now also rewriting the script himself. ("I can't do a movie without running it through my typewriter myself," he said.) May's contributions could be detected in the soap opera scenes. She fleshed out the characters of Sandy Lester and John Van Horn, and invented the character of Michael's playwright-roommate, Jeff. She also helped Sydney develop his commitment to the notion that *Tootsie* was about a man impersonating a woman and thereby becoming a better man.

Robert Garland, who had written *The Electric Horseman* which Pollack had directed in 1979, replaced May for a short time; then May returned to work *à trois* with him and Sydney. Later on during the filming, Valerie Curtin and Barry Levinson, co-authors of *Best Friends*, did a brief stint, making suggestions on the script.

When the movie commenced shooting in April, Sydney was still working on the script with his writers and Dustin was once again working on the script with Murray Schisgal. Almost $1½ million had been spent on literary talent, and yet the script continued to change.

"We always have our big fights on Monday," Sydney commented. That was because all weekend, each man had been working on the script. They would each come in with pages; close the door behind them; thrash out their differences. Since characters were changing, casting was delayed. Since lines were changing, it was impossible to rehearse as much as Dustin would have liked *before* the shoot began.

"You know what's hard about movies?" Dustin said during the soap opera shoot. "It's that you've got to start it in two weeks and you don't really have the time to fuck around." He turned to Sydney. "Ideally you would be in a rehearsal room with the actors and you would be there directing the actors and you would be . . . fucking around for *two months!*"

As the first assistant director, in charge of the set and all its people and their efficiency, David McGiffert felt disabled by the unresolved state of the *Tootsie* script. A good-looking Californian with a perpetual tan and exhausted eyes, he often had no answers to give the waiting crew and seemed to lug the resultant morale problems around on his head like part of his headset.

"There's an ideal way to make a movie," he said. "And that's when the script is locked in before you start. So that when you scout locations and hire actors, you'll know *where* they'll be saying what is written and *what is written doesn't change.* With this movie . . . up to the time we started shooting, we were working blind. We had a compilation of I think four scripts that were synthesized and the best things culled and put together. The characters changed. The nuances of scenes changed. In some cases, the locations changed while we were shooting and that makes it very insecure for everybody."

At the wrap party in late August, Bill Lucek, the scenic charge-man, and Peter Larkin, the production designer, would joke about how Larkin had often come to the set shop from production meetings with schedules that were worthless within hours. Because as the script changed, the locations changed. They rented a dance studio because in one version of the script, that's where Michael Dorsey was living. Then suddenly, no more dance studio. Michael Dorsey was living in a partitioned loft. And the scenic artists suddenly found themselves building walls through the middle of the dance studio. "There were days when it was 5:30," Larkin recalled, "and you didn't know where to tell people to be the next day, and by 7:30, you were ready to shoot the scene in a clothes closet."

Even Owen Roizman, the cinematographer whose lack of insecurity was legend on the *Tootsie* set, felt unsettled and dis-advantaged by the lack of a final guiding text.

"When I do a picture normally," he said unhappily, "I read the script several times before I start and when it reaches production, I go over it personally and mark it very carefully to figure what transitions I'm going to make photographically. In other words . . . it depends on style . . . but for example, if there are scenes that play a certain time of day and then at other times, I want to make subtle transitions in the way that I expose the film or the way I light a shot, to make it feel like the same day; later in the day—things like that. I usually have it very well laid out and very carefully planned. And if you asked me a question about the script, I could tell you which page it was on and who said what and where. I'd even suggest lines sometimes. I mean I don't *like* to do that because I don't like to be a pain-in-the-ass. But I do like to contribute something. But in this movie I couldn't do it. Because of all the changes, inputs and different pages coming in every day. I stopped looking at the script very early in the picture. Because it was useless. Dustin would come up with new pages. He and Sydney would argue about it. They'd end up compromising somewhere. And I couldn't plan anything ahead of time. I decided to go on the memory I had of the script I had read. And on my feelings—on that day—of what to do. And that's the way I've gone through the picture."

In easier times, crew members would recall the scriptless tension of the early shoot with real wonder. Most of them had never lived through anything like it on any movie. The star and the director were closed in a room, arguing about a line, a scene; no one could mediate between them; no one could hasten their agreement; *no one could move until they agreed.* When they had finally settled on a compromise, the doors would open, the script would be revised and the movie would surge forward with sudden speed and no time to prepare.

"You feel as though there's this train on its way somewhere," David McGiffert said, "and you'd just better jump on and grab a seat and hope it gets wherever it's going."

On a morning in July, Dustin and Sydney were having one of their discussions. Ann Egbert, the Directors Guild trainee, was poised outside Dustin's dressing room, waiting. David McGiffert was out at the set, waiting.

"Annie?" he said softly to her through his headset.

"Nothing yet," the young woman answered through hers.

The discussion that day was about a conversation between Julie and Dorothy.

Julie is being indecisive about her love life. And her friend Dorothy, the Southern homespun philosopher, is supposed to say: "Why plant sorghum when grits is what you want?"

Julie finally makes up her mind. And she is supposed to say to Dorothy: "Like you always say, a child that don't ask don't get no grits."

Dustin wanted these lines out.

Sydney thought they were funny.

Dustin agreed they might be funny, but since Dorothy had never used Southern homespun philosopher expressions before in the movie, he didn't think she should suddenly start now.

"But you're *inferring*," Sydney insisted. "The wonderful thing about movies is that you can infer that there was some night when Dorothy got caught and started spouting these Southern expressions, and Julie remembered."

Dustin said that inference couldn't work because we had not *heard* Dorothy do grits-talk before; we had not *seen* her Southern disguise developed to the idiomatic stage.

And Sydney tried to convince Dustin.

And Dustin insisted on convincing Sydney.

And Ann Egbert reported to David McGiffert that there was "nothing yet."

And finally, the lines were dropped.

In fact, the argument had not really concerned a couple of lines; it had concerned literality in film, and losing it bothered Sydney.

"I don't like it through a mirror," he said. "I like it through a *prism*. We write and write and it's 170 pages. *Everything* is covered, it's way too long. Then you take fifty pages out and it's better. It's *better*. Because the stuff that you have taken out has *dripped colors* on the stuff that's left. It happens in the editing too. You take a scene out that you swear is essential, but the people are playing the next scene as though they already played that scene, so when you take it out, you've got something inferred and not literal life."

Sydney swung back in his executive swing chair; his wide, thin mouth had tightened to a straight line; the springs beneath him groaned. Suddenly he bounced upright, threw up his big hands and sighed with grandiose acceptance. He had decided to relax. He would chew gum. Eat a peach. Go on to the next item.

"It's impossible to work in comedy when there's bad blood and bad air," he said. "I can only try to persuade him. If I push it, I've got a stubborn, angry actor trying to do something he doesn't believe in, and I can't win with that. It's okay for me to be uptight, but it's not okay for him because he has to be in front of the camera and people will see it."

He swiveled back to the typewriter, where the incessantly rewritten script dangled, and started trying to figure out how the scene could be rewritten without "grits-talk."

II

TONY MARRERO, THE HAIR stylist for Dorothy Michaels, kept a drawerful of stills from early camera tests that were part of a monumental effort to help Dustin Hoffman look like a real woman. There were stills of Dustin in every type and style of wig and base and powder, every cut and color of dress. Dustin blonde and Dustin dusky. Dustin chic and Dustin dowdy.

This painstaking search for the "right" Dorothy extended beyond make-up and wardrobe to gait and voice. It unearthed Dorothy's history and background, and conditioned the way she appeared to other people in the film and finally determined the way she was funny to the audience. The question that Dustin wanted answered was simply: "What if I had been born a woman? What kind of woman would I be? . . . There's only one way you're gonna look believable as a woman, I mean, we didn't have ten choices. We wanted *the one way*—and once you found that, then you started to look at the rushes and then you could say: Now *that's* me." He laughed. "I guess."

To create that single breakthrough concept cost hundreds of thousands of dollars and made make-up a life-and-death issue for *Tootsie*. "The first thing I said," Dustin remembered, "is that we have to do a bunch of make-up tests until we arrive at myself looking like a woman. Let's see if I can look really believable, not camp, not uglified, not denigrated . . . Because if I were a woman, I'd want to look as attractive as possible."

Allen Weisinger, the make-up artist who inherited both the problem and its solution, could only really guess at its history. A stocky man with a tawny beard, he wore a little blue apron with pockets for brushes and powder and vials over his khaki shorts. He looked like he were going to an archaeological dig, and followed Dorothy Michaels around, dusting her chin and her cheeks, fixing her lipstick, as though she were a priceless piece of antique statuary. To counteract the tensions of his job, Allen played tennis out in New Jersey against opponents who were invariably younger and looser than he was. He smoked Marlboros. He went on a diet together with Les Lazarowitz, the sound mixer. Whoever lost more weight by the end of the shoot would collect the difference in pounds from the other, at $100 a pound.

"Hoffman had a twenty year relationship with [make-up artist] Dick Smith," Allen said in a quiet interval while Dorothy was rehearsing. "They'd done major films together." (*Little Big Man* was one in which Dustin aged from childhood to over 120 years, playing a gunslinger, a drunk, a witness to the Wounded Knee massacre, a cavalry scout, virtually every role available in the Old West. It was a make-up tour de force.) "So naturally with a movie like this," Allen continued, "Hoffman went back to Smith.

"Smith consulted, did tests, and developed the teeth (with David Shelby, an artist/dentist). The teeth are a very important part of the look. Dustin's teeth are irregular and masculine in their irregularity. Women generally have more even teeth and also (they are) slightly curved because the mouth is smaller. If I do a complete make-up and don't put in the teeth and he smiles, it looks like drag. And what we tried to do is not look like drag. *Drag is death!*"

After Sydney came on as director and *Tootsie* stopped just testing and started really rolling, George Masters took over make-up. Masters specialized in making beautiful women even more beautiful. He gave

Dorothy the same eyes he had designed for Bo Derek and Ann-Margret. Dustin told Rocky Lang, the young filmmaker who was shooting a documentary about *Tootsie*, that he felt sure Masters' make-up "really was the breakthrough."

However, the make-up sometimes took three and four hours to apply, and when it was finally on, Dustin was already exhausted, with only a few hours of acting energy left. And the make-up wasn't consistent. One day, Dustin seemed bluer than the next day. One day he looked shinier ("hotter," they say on movie sets) than the day before.

Dustin's beard was the real killer. He has a black beard that grows with normal haste. So he would rise extra early in the morning, shave (up, not down) in a sauna because the pore-opening heat allowed him to shave closer than usual, settle into the chair and have make-up applied to his skin for hours. By the time he was ready to work, the beard was on its way back, and there were only so many hours left in the working day before it would make its dark appearance on Dorothy Michael's pert face and make Dustin look like he was in drag. And drag, as Allen Weisinger had said, was death.

"The make-up was so thick (to cover the beard) that Dustin could only be lit very flatly," Owen Roizman said. ("Flatly" meant straight white light with no modelling.) "And in shooting movies, that's almost impossible to get all the time, because people move around a room, in shadows . . . and you should be able to light whatever the scene dictates."

Besides lighting problems, the make-up was creating health and well-being problems for an actor who has as much energy as anyone in show business. Dustin was having to shave his legs; his arms; the backs of his fingers. His eyebrows were bleached. As a kid he had suffered from what he had once called "the worst case of acne in Los Angeles" and now the nightmare was returning. He was getting rashes; pimples; his skin was literally hurting. He already had one pair of lifts stuck to his face to pull the skin taut. But two weeks before shooting started, he had lost so much weight that new lines and configurations on his face necessitated an additional pair of lifts, and heavy make-up to cover them.

Somehow, with all the testing, Dustin had never actually been photographed next to other middle-aged women. And when he sat among them while rehearsing the audition for the soap opera, he just didn't look as womanly as many had hoped.

It tore up the morale of the set, as any midstream artistic personnel change would, but George Masters left *Tootsie*.

Dorothy Pearl, whom Jessica Lange had brought on as her personal make-up artist, reworked Dorothy's make-up. She was credited with solving the consistency problem. Dorothy Michaels began to look more like the same woman at each day's rushes, although in the final film, trained eyes could still detect differences in the way Dorothy looked in the soap opera scenes, for example (which were shot early in the filming), and the scenes in Julie's apartment, which were shot later. Pearl changed some of the base materials and whittled down the time it took to put Dorothy Michaels' face in place. Therefore, Dustin could spend less time "in the chair," and more time on the set—although the beard watch never stopped.

Since Jessica would not authorize Pearl to make up Dustin on a regular basis, Weisinger was hired. He followed Pearl's scheme, which had inherited and preserved major elements from both Smith and Masters. With practice, he reduced "chair time" even more, and found a fast way to take off the lifts at lunchtime so Dustin could actually relax for an hour before the lifts had to go on again.

Still, however, there were unresolved difficulties.

"We had never shot exteriors," Allen said. "We had to learn how to stipple more red into the make-up so it would look passable in blue light (outdoors) as well as tungsten light (indoors). Owen figured that you had to pour more light on Dustin because his make-up absorbed so much light. So that if you had Dustin sitting next to somebody else . . . you needed more light to bring Dustin up to the same reflective value as the person with normal make-up on."

Allen would hover on the fringes of every Dorothy scene, nervous that the lifts on Dustin's face would come up because of sweat from the heat of the lights. Snap, there goes a jowl. Pop, down comes an eyebrow. Work fast, here comes the beard.

To Peter Larkin, the production designer, the absolute control of light demanded by Dorothy's make-up seemed to spell the elimination of natural outdoor light from the movie's interior shots. A droll, dark-humored man who was well-known in the theatre for his design of such shows as *Teahouse of the August Moon* and more recently *Dancin'*, he had looked forward to reality of lighting in the movie. But it was not to be his, not in *Tootsie*. "There you are on the twenty-sixth floor," he sighed, "with all of New York before you, and they're covering up the windows."

One critical element in Dorothy Michaels' disguise was her glasses. First of all, they augmented the physical barrier between the look of Dustin as Dorothy and the look of Dustin as Michael Dorsey. Secondly, they diminished the size of Dustin's nose, and added to the no-nonsense, professional quality Dorothy needed to get the soap opera role of Emily Kimberly.

"Glasses: I hate 'em," Owen Roizman said. "They're a nightmare. Every time they ask me if somebody should wear glasses, I say 'No! Get 'cm off!' "

Originally, when he was using flat light, the sources of light had to be large and close to the camera. The reflection problem with Dorothy's glasses was, therefore, severe and needed solving. Sydney recalled that the late Bob Gottschalk, then head of Panavision, had once told him about a special coating which could be sprayed on camera lenses to make them non-reflective. This same material could be sprayed on glasses, to diminish the impression of thickness. George Burns had used it to good effect, Gottschalk said; maybe, Sydney thought, Dorothy Michaels could too.

So Dorothy's glasses were sprayed. And the glare was gone. "We put a little bit of oil on the glasses to make them shine just enough for you to know they're there," Sydney said. "But otherwise, no reflection."

"I'm putting that in my little book," Owen said.

Ron Schwary, a tough, cheerful producer from Portland, translated the make-up problems and the script problems directly into time, and thence into dollars. Schwary had produced *Ordinary People*; he had been executive producer on *Absence of Malice* (and actually portrays a Broadway producer in *Tootsie*), and he fretted about how the script and make-up hassles would look on the daily production reports that recorded every minute's activity—and in-activity—for the information of the studio.

"A lot of money was spent to prepare this picture when it wasn't ready to shoot," he said. "Look . . . Sydney comes in in December of '81. They start doing make-up tests *again* in L.A. so they go for a February shooting start. But the script isn't ready. The make-up isn't right after all. They need more pre-shoot rehearsal time. So they put it off for March 8th. Then 15th. Finally the first of April.

"If we budgeted wrong, and scheduled wrong, it was because we couldn't get a full day's work in because of the make-up."

Sydney himself explained to *Variety* the following September that at least two of the 23 days *Tootsie* went over schedule were spent in reshooting and new screen tests, necessitated by changes in the make-up.

By the time Dorothy Michaels' make-up was perfected, company morale had taken a bad beating. Sydney Pollack was by his own admission "up tight," more easily angered than those who knew him had ever seen him. Dustin's nerves were rubbed as raw as his skin; his perfectionism had made him a willing victim of the make-up hassles, but by now, "the chair" was his least favorite location.

There he sat, at 8 o'clock in the morning at National Video in July, with Allen working on him and Dorothy Michaels emerging from his face. "It was supposed to be six weeks of Dorothy make-ups," he said. "And now it's the *sixteenth* week! They're torture. They're getting worse every day. I'm starting to get phobic about them."

Allen worked fast, concentrated as a surgeon under the gun. Dustin's black hair had been flattened against his head by a stocking cap. In his faded blue terry cloth robe, with all that black around his eyes and all that goo on his skin, he looked like Marat before the fateful bath. The hair that awaited him—Dorothy Michaels' auburn curls—sat on a faceless head under a dryer in Tony Marrero's space across the hall.

"I shaved my legs," Dustin told Rocky Lang. "The hair is growing back. I've got rashes. I've been scratching. I begin to say to myself: If I was a woman, *I would not shave*, man! I just wouldn't do it. Why do I have to aggravate my skin? Because men go 'Uck' when they see hair under an armpit?! I don't think men have really any idea the discomfort women go through to please us unless they shave their armpits, shave their legs . . ."

Next to Dustin's mirror, there was a large calendar. On it, the dread Dorothy make-ups were marked off with big red Xs—kind of like a menstrual period.

. . .

"Get Ruth Morley in here," Dustin said. "It's Ruth Morley and I
on the end of *Kramer* that's the real genesis of *Tootsie*."

Ruth Morley, the costume designer, an energetic woman with a
brilliant smile who loved to wear purple clothes, flopped down on
the sofa. Ruth had come to this country as a child from Austria. She
exhuded a joyousness that often characterizes those who have been
snatched from the worst of times. Her laugh was catching. She had
received an Academy Award nomination for *The Miracle Worker*
and her costume designs for *Annie Hall* had made a memorable impact on American fashion.

"One of the things Ruth and I were trying to do," Dustin continued, "was to feminize Ted Kramer more."

Feminize politically?

"Oh no," they both answered. "Feminize physically. And emotionally."

"Because he started out as this vain advertising man and he became more and more a mother," Ruth said.

"And he started out as a guy who wasn't even a father," Dustin
said.

"I got a shirt," Ruth recalled, "which was really a woman's shirt
[but only she and Dustin knew that] and a bag, we called it 'the
mother bag' for when he went to the park, you know one of those
bags with all the junk in it, the toys and the bottles and the
juices . . ."

"I wrote a lot of my stuff on the stand [in the brilliant courtroom
custody case scenes in *Kramer*], Dustin continued. "I shouldn't say
I wrote, I mean improvised . . . I liked one of the takes in the rushes
where I get emotional and I break down with the judge and in
breaking down I get lost and I say: 'I get up when he does, I give
him breakfast, I take him to school, I bring him home at night, I
bring him dinner, I'm his mother!' And they say, 'No, you're his
father.' I say: 'No! I'm his *mother*! He didn't come out of my vagina
but I'm his mother!' And there was a moment on the stand when I
could smell it, like an animal, smell that I was gonna lose the kid,
and it's very emotional for me. I'm going through a separation at the

28

time (from his first wife, Anne) and *it's the first time* that what I'm doing as an actor corresponds to what is going on in my life.

"That's what every artist does. They create something in their art out of the moment in their lives.

"And people said: 'That must have been very hard for you.' And I said: 'No, it's a *joy*! *To be able to get it out*. It's what I wish I could do all the time!' "

"So," he said, "after the movie's over, I'm walking around and I'm having these conversations with my best friend Murray Schisgal and he's saying: 'Well, what would you like to do next?' I'm saying: 'I'd like to work like I worked on *Kramer* . . . it wasn't the *facts* of my life but it was more or less the *truth* of it.'

"I almost started to touch something in that movie, almost started to touch something, and that is the woman inside of us, what Murray and I referred to as 'Shirley'. And I'm suddenly thinking, I never thought it before, *what if* I had been born a woman instead of a man? The same genetic structure. The same parents. Basically the same looks . . ."

But a woman. A woman who is himself.

Given this passion—for *personal truth* in the creation of Dorothy —Ruth Morley's job involved much more than merely the outfitting of a character in a movie. She already knew that Dustin's clothes would have to be selected with attention to their subliminal impact on his state of mind, for that was the way she had worked with him on *Kramer*. The costume was not a costume; it was a casing of support right next to the skin of an artist who was trying to find a whole new world *inside* himself by spinning a whole new skin *outside* himself.

"I like working with actors who *care* more than with actors who say 'Put something on me,' " Ruth said. "And when they care (as much as Dustin cared about his costume), I let the actor wear it home. In *Taxi Driver*, when I finally found *the* plaid shirt Bobby (De Niro) wanted to wear, when I found the army jacket, the pants, well, *he wanted to wear them*. Some wardrobe people would get hysterical. They'd say: 'You can't let him take it home and live in it!' But I say: 'Look, if he really wants to live in it for a while, *sleep* in it, let him!' . . . I knew that with Bobby, there was no question that he could lose it or do anything to it. *He loved it too much*."

Dustin's immersion in character was no less demanding than De Niro's. Dustin had mastered Italian to play a romantic bank clerk in *Alfredo, Alfredo*. He had visited jails to prepare *Straight Time*. If he was going to play an actress in *Tootsie*, then he was going to become a clothes horse like an actress, and his request to Ruth Morley was that he wanted "to look as pretty and feminine as possible at all times."

"There are really three characters on Dustin's back in this film," Ruth explained. "I tried to keep them all separate. So the problem was not just to make him look like a woman, but two different women, with different clothes coming from the minds of their creators. Michael Dorsey created Dorothy Michaels. But a bunch of soap opera writers created Emily Kimberly."

Emily wore what the soap opera wardrobe people gave her . . . which in this case was "tough cookie" suits. The costume staff had been delighted that the role Dorothy was to play in the soap opera had evolved out of nurse into hospital administrator. First of all, it gave Dorothy much more range as a character. And besides, a nurse couldn't believably wear high necked collars. And Dustin, with his 16½ inch neck and prominent Adam's apple, *had* to wear high necked collars. Ruth was glad furthermore not to have to continue worrying about "all that make-up and all that white."

Unlike Emily's outfits, Dorothy's clothes evolved, for they were being assembled by a man whose financial life was changing swiftly. "In the beginning," Ruth said, "when Michael first goes out to shop (for Dorothy's clothes), he has no money."

So in one of the movie's most memorable scenes, he hits on George Fields, his agent. George is trying to have lunch in the Russian Tea Room when this aggressive southern flounce snuggles up to him and horrifies him by saying in a familiar strangulated baritone, "It's me, George, me, Michael."

With the $1000 George advances him, Michael goes out and buys Dorothy something to wear. That first shopping trip is an eye-opener for Michael, who marvels to his friend Jeff how any woman can afford to keep herself reasonably attractive in today's market.

But as Dorothy's performances take hold, and the show's ratings start going up, with 2000 fan letters a week coming in for Dorothy

Michaels, the actress's contract is renewed, with a big raise. "So when Michael goes shopping later in the movie," Ruth Morley continued, "he's buying for a rich successful dame."

This dame turned out to be a Southerner. Soft, romantic, Blanche du Bois clothes suited her. The wide brimmed ante-bellum hat she wore for her weekend up at the farm won the old-fashioned heart of Charles Durning. Her jewelry improved too. "Atlanta Hadassah," Dustin growled at her in his mirror.

Turtlenecks, Ruth Morley began to see, flattered Dustin less because they outlined his brawny neck and made him look masculine. The cowl neck sweater was a logical alternative, and he wore one for his first day on the job at the soap. But the body of it was too loose and floppy to suit his trim figure. A gored skirt was good because he had a tiny behind (which was augmented by padded panty hose) and, it turned out, terrific legs.

"He got to love his waistline," Ruth laughed. "A twenty-seven inch waist! I wish I had it!"

Flashy high heels were forbidden to Dorothy because they were the traditional footwear of drag queens. Ruth got Dustin's shoes at Coward's, where more conservative styles could be had in sizes wide enough for his feet.

"I thought I would have more trouble walking in high heels than I did," Dustin remembered. "I just did what I do when I ski . . . kind of hug the ground with the toe . . . If I were a woman, I would never wear them."

As for breasts, Ruth said, "Dustin wanted real big ones." She urged him to modify his desires downward toward something ample but not grotesque on his small frame. In the unlimited resources of New York's many underworlds, she found a woman who supplied the transvestite community, and who actually conducted classes on how to walk and act like a woman. From this and other advisors, she solicited manifold breast suggestions. Like rice-filled falsies. ("They bounce," Ruth said.) And falsies filled with bird seed. ("My big fear of course was that when he began to sweat, his bosom would grow oats.")

She had falsies made up that were stuffed with the tiny circles of foam used for packing. These could be seen floating around the dressing room. Sticking to things and people. She ended up with a custom-fitted pair from a store that makes post-mastectomy prostheses. They cost $175 each.

"Originally," Ruth said, "it was supposed to be a winter film. And when he got off the train in Kingston (to visit Julie and Les for Christmas), Dorothy was supposed to look like Anna Karenina."

But with all the delays, the shoot started in April. That changed a Christmas weekend to an Easter weekend and finally to a plain old weekend. It eliminated heavy sweaters and plush coats which might have covered Dustin more completely. Suddenly Ruth and her staff found themselves making blouses and skirts. Since Ruth was responsible for the design and look of every single person in the movie, including all the extras, she and Jennifer Nichols, head of women's wardrobe, could be seen in a worried huddle in the days before the outdoor filming of Dorothy Michaels' first foray into the streets of Manhattan. Dorothy would be on her way to audition for the role of Emily Kimberly. She would be observing other women in the street. When they hitched their shoulder bags, she would hitch hers. She would be imitating their stance, their stride, trying not to trip in her moderately high heels. It would be early March in the movie.

Except, of course, it would *really* be mid-July, with the temperature in the 90's. Dustin would be dripping beneath his long sleeves; his high collar; his auburn curls. No ordinary passers-by would be allowed to pass by him, because they would be stripped down for the heat. "So we'll have to use extras," Ruth sighed good-naturedly. "At six in the morning, Sylvia's best. (Sylvia Fay handled extra casting.) That means the ones who have already been beaten and read the riot act. None of these untrained people who say, 'It's ninety-four degrees and you want me to wear a coat?!' "

In her earliest visions of Dorothy, Ruth Morley had planned for Dustin's preferred blues and greens and her own preferred mauves and purples. However, every costume decision—like every make-up choice—had to get past Sydney and Owen Roizman. Sydney said that Owen's great strength as a cinematographer was precisely his ability to make less than perfect women like Dorothy Michaels "look as pretty and feminine as possible at all times." And Owen suggested that because of the very fast film he was using and the tendency of Dorothy's make-up to look blue under the heavy light, warmer colors —reds, browns, oranges—would be preferable.

So Michael Dorsey dressed in blue and green.

And Dorothy Michaels looked like autumn.

Unlike her make-up and wardrobe, so arduously tested and planned, Dorothy Michaels' *voice* was the product of inspiration. In the early scripts, Dorothy had no particular ethnic background. But Dustin was looking for a voice for Dorothy, and "with the Southern accent," Sydney recalled, "it was easier to pitch his voice up."

Dustin consulted a speech therapist. He and Sydney went to Columbia University. Dustin watched the graphs made by an oscilloscope print of a woman's voice, so that he could see the lines he would have to make to achieve a feminine pitch. He found that if he used a French accent, that automatically raised the pitch. "But he speaks French in falsetto," Sydney told Janet Maslin of the *New York Times*, "and that wouldn't have worked." The Southern accent won out, and for coaching in it, Dustin sought help from Polly Holliday.

Once Dorothy *spoke* like a Southerner, all the people who were working on her could begin to supply the bits and pieces of background that Bob Evans had so missed in the earliest versions of *Tootsie*, and her character began to crystallize.

She became a lady: well-mannered, somewhat formal.

"If you asked me what I thought Dustin Hoffman would be like as a woman," Sydney said, "I would say probably pretty brassy, kind of vulgar, sort of loud. And instead, he's this very proper, *extremely* proper middle-aged Southern belle. Now how this came out this way, I don't know . . . and neither does he."

The "Shirley" inside Dustin Hoffman was turning out to be a fascinating stranger.

"Sydney was very good at the screen tests," Dustin said. "He started to improvise with me and stuff just started to come out. . . ."

"The other day at the improvisation," Sydney said, "I said, you're a wonderful lady, Miss Michaels, you're terribly pretty and terribly proper, but I have difficulty figuring out how to approach you as a man. I mean . . . my instinct would be to be terribly careful with you."

And Dustin pondered. And Dorothy said: "Well, maybe I've done that deliberately to keep men at their distance."

If an actress is keeping men at their distance, that immediately evokes suspicion. What's she hiding? What's her story? And if you know you're under suspicion, and that one wrong answer could blow your cover, you listen very carefully to everything everybody asks you. "It's a combination of the accent and sort of leaning forward emotionally," Sydney said. "He needs to hear you, to get the question from you, 'cause he's scared he won't be able to answer it . . . and as he does that, he gets very feminine."

Dabney Coleman as Ron, the womanizing soap director, finds Dorothy mysterious because she finds him resistible. Maybe she's gay . . . no, maybe not. . . .

John Van Horn, the sex-crazed senior physician played by George Gaynes, finds Dorothy mysterious because she tries to avoid kissing him on the soap. So he looks beyond her glasses and discovers her beautiful Bo Derek eyes and finally, wild with curiosity and lust, follows her home to her oddly junky apartment. She resists. He insists. Jeff enters. Ah, that's why she resisted! She has a lover!

Julie, too, is curious about Dorothy.

One night, when Dorothy comes over for dinner, she asks: "Were you ever married, Dorothy?"

"Oh no, I was never that fortunate," Dorothy answers. Michael under her wig is very nervous because he's going to have to make this up as he goes along. And the more nervous he gets, the more prim Dorothy gets, and the more prim she is, the more heartbreak Julie assumes her to be hiding.

"I was once engaged to a brilliant young actor," Dorothy says, "whose career was unfortunately cut short by the insensitivity of the Theatrical Establishment."

"They killed him!" Julie gasps.

"In a manner of speaking," Dorothy responds crisply. "Sutton gave up acting and me as well and is now a waiter working in a disreputable restaurant."

So now, Michael was making up Dorothy out of material from his own life, and the more he did that, the more organic the role became to Dustin Hoffman, who does that too.

Having established Dorothy's persona as Southern, prim, and ladylike, it remained for *Tootsie* to create situations in which that combination would make her famous and also funny. "At first we felt she would become famous by great acting," Dustin said. "But

34

you can't really do great acting as Emily Kimberly in the soap stuff, I mean, you can't. So then, well, how do you become famous? Maybe you don't become famous by great acting. Maybe you become famous for screwing around with the text so that you do little mischievous or outrageous things that make an audience look up. So that when she's supposed to say something rather gentle to Dr. Brewster, she hits him over the head. . . . When you start behaving physically as a man, while people are thinking you're a woman, then that suddenly gets attention."

Thus, some of the funniest moments in *Tootsie* occur when Dorothy suddenly acts like a man.

She flounces out of Les' farm pickup truck with her ruffled skirt and forgets how dainty she's supposed to be and easily hoists her own suitcases. "Let me do that," Les offers gallantly. But when he takes the bag, he can hardly lift it.

Dorothy is laden with packages from a big shopping trip. She hails a cab. A man with a briefcase lunges in front of her and steals the cab. She physically throws him out of the taxi and his briefcase after him.

If Michael Dorsey had acted that way, no one would have laughed. If Dorothy Michaels had been a brassy vulgar type and acted that way, no one would have laughed. When *a real woman* acts that way, no one cracks a smile. The comedy was in the slapstick; but the *heart* of the comedy was in the success of Dorothy's disguise.

Dustin worked and developed Dorothy's material even when he was off camera. Between takes, he would play Dorothy with the crew. He blew kisses. He flirted.

"I operate like most men," he said. "I'm just as perfunctory as the next guy in terms of showing physical affection. Maybe I'm a little more emotional because I'm an actor, I don't know. But I know when I put on the woman's outfit, when I'm with the crew, I'm very physical. I go put my arms around them. I flirt."

One of Dustin's favorite foils in the flirting game was Bobby Wilson, a large, gentle man with a grey moustache and twinkling eyes, who did props on *Tootsie*. "Ladies and gentleman," Dustin announced in Dorothy's sweet voice, "I want you to meet my fiancé, Bobby. He's a wonderful man. Lost his wife a few years ago. I was his first date since then. We haven't consummated it yet, though, have we Bobby?"

"We will though," Wilson answered gruffly. "We're going to Puerto Rico."

"We are?! Well!" Dorothy placed her hand upon her breast in what became a characteristic gesture and tilted her head toward her listeners confidentially. "He's so easy to satisfy. I mean, when I got to be my age, I never thought I'd be . . . I mean . . . I'm flabbergasted . . . every time I look at him, I'm in awe, I mean . . . he's everything I've always wanted. You know how safe I feel walking down the streets of New York since I've been engaged to Bobby?" The crew cracked up. Bobby cracked up. But not Dorothy. She pursed her red lips and patted her curls. She could go on forever. One day she'd complain of menstrual cramps. Another day she'd admit to all present that she was having sexual fantasies about Al Pacino. "I was putting on my make-up this morning," she told Rocky Lang, "and I was thinking of all the roles I could do, and there is this wonderful part in *The Importance of Being Earnest*; you know . . . the aunt. I could do a little Blanche in *Streetcar*. Linda in *Death of a Salesman*."

In the film, Michael Dorsey tells George Fields that now that he's established as Dorothy, he could play Medea! Eleanor Roosevelt! He could do a television special! He's got something to say to women!

"You haven't got anything to say to women, Michael," George answers. "You're not like other women. You're a man."

But Michael Dorsey has come to believe that Dorothy has something to say to women because Dorothy used to be an out-of-work actor. And it is possible that the insecurity of the actor, who knows what it's like to wait by the phone for twenty years, parallels the insecurity of the woman who is less than pretty, who has waited by a few silent phones herself.

Dustin explained how he had pulled this truth from his own life and imprinted it on the character of Dorothy.

"I always thought I got cast in *The Graduate*," he said, "because I was one of the last ones to be seen. I said to Mike Nichols on the phone, look, I'm Jewish. Italian. I'm not this Benjamin Braddock. I mean we were just talking then, you don't know you're talking about a big hit, you're just talking, and in New York, I'm getting scripts now, I'm doing better than I've ever done in my life, Kerr says I'm as funny in *Eh* as Buster Keaton, I was feeling wonderful.

"Nichols said over the phone: 'Benjamin is Jewish inside.'

"Nichols . . . brought me out to California to test and I was sitting in the make-up chair and I felt like the absolute ugliest piece of shit there ever was.

"I mean, I always felt like that but this time was worse.

"And Nichols kept saying: 'What are we going to *do* with him?!'

. . . and they plucked my eyebrows and pulled out the hairs from my nose and he kept saying, 'What are we going to *do* about his nose?!' He wanted me to look as good as I could. He'd seen me read. He knew I could act. He wanted me . . . I went back to *Eh* after the screen test and said, 'Don't worry about nothin', folks. I'll be here. I ain't getting that job.' "

(Hoffman laughed. The desert days of rejection are so real to him that his voice describing them had ground to a dry rasp.)

"I later saw the screen test," he said. Laughing. "I was terrible."

(He can laugh because, of course, he got the role, terrible screen test or not, and it made him a star.)

"I mean Nichols was very pressured," Hoffman said. "In those days I don't think there was an average looking or homely looking person playing romantic leads. I mean Alan Arkin had done *The Russians Are Coming* but that wasn't a romantic lead. No other director would have cast me, *no other*."

There is a scene in *Tootsie* in which Michael Dorsey, the actor, tries to explain to his roommate Jeff his desperate frustration because, no matter how he dresses Dorothy, how he fixes her hair, her eyes, he *cannot* make her more beautiful. And he is almost crying, that's how frustrated he is, because he wants her to be beautiful and she just won't be!

Every woman who has ever looked with a truthful eye into an unyielding mirror has felt what Michael Dorsey feels at that moment.

But Michael Dorsey, remember, is Dustin Hoffman.

"This movie's a comedy but this character makes me cry . . .," Dustin told Gene Siskel of the *Chicago Tribune*. "She doesn't have a man. She never got married. She never had kids. And it hurts me 'cause she's not pretty. She doesn't meet the criteria (of physical beauty) that I don't need as a man. And I work off that. And nobody knows it. Nobody knows it but she moves me. I know her. I *know* her."

One day on the set of *Southwest General*, Ron—who sometimes calls Dorothy "Tootsie"—calls her "Tootsie" once too often. She whirls on him, irate. "My name is Dorothy!" she snaps. "It's not 'Tootsie' or 'Toots' or 'Sweetie' or 'Honey' or 'Doll'."

"Oh, Christ," Ron says.

"No," says Dorothy, "just Dorothy. Now Alan is always Alan. Tom's always Tom and John's always John. I have a name, too. It's Dorothy. Capital D.O.R.O.T.H.Y. Dorothy."

Jennifer Nichols remembered watching the scene, watching Dorothy fighting back bitter tears of frustration. "Oh Dusty," she said, "that's it, that's just what we go through, that's just how we feel."

Perhaps Dustin Hoffman could rend that recognition from women not because he was dressed like one of them, but because he could remember—with his powerful affective memory—he could remember the pain of feeling like "the absolute ugliest piece of shit there ever was."

Dorothy Michaels becomes such a rage as Emily Kimberly that national magazines begin demanding her face and her body for their pages.

So, on August 6th, the "Famous Fashion Shoot" happened. It would end up as a graphic montage in the final film, with Dustin in all Dorothy's high fashion outfits leaping from the cover of *Newsweek* to the cover of *Cosmopolitan* to the cover of *Ms.*, and it would take less than a minute in screen time. But it took a full day to shoot.

As shooting goes, this was an easy day, with only one set-up (movie people call it "one deal")—Dorothy Michaels modelling clothes against a white paper background. Outside the loft on 18th Street, the Teamsters played cards in the row of Ryder trucks that carried the movie around New York. The local hamburger joints in this print-and-paper neighborhood had put bright magic-markered signs in their windows, welcoming *Tootsie* to their lunch counters.

A festive mood reached from the street into the loft; it was Friday; respite was near; and it wasn't too hot.

The loft was full of gorgeous clothes, and photographers. The wise-cracking Brian Hamill, unit still photographer for *Tootsie*, was there as always, exchanging boxing stories with Dustin. However, free lance photographers had been invited in today as well. And Greg Gorman, who had come to New York originally to take publicity pictures of *Tootsie* for Columbia, was retained to appear *in the movie* as a photographer taking pictures of Dorothy.

"Where's my black bra?" Dustin called in Dorothy's sweet voice. Jennifer Nichols and Franke Piazza, Dustin's wardrobe man, produced it. Soon he appeared on the white paper background in a slinky black number and the crew whistled.

"Big smile, Dorothy," Greg called. Do it this way, Dusty, Tony Marrero said. Do it that way, Dusty, Franke Piazza said. Sydney Pollack laughed, bunched up his long legs, laid an electronic keyboard across his lap and toodled Latin rhythms. A player-by-ear, self-taught, he had mastered the way chords are organized within keys and with a little hunting and pecking could play the basics.

"I'm heating up," Dorothy announced, twisting, turning, preening, slinking.

Jennifer put her into a floor length Ben Kahn lynx coat. Few men or women on the set failed to cop a feel. "Snuggle down in that coat," Sydney called, wriggling his lanky frame. "Make love to that coat," Greg called.

Kas Self, Dustin's stand-in, stood near the camera just watching. "I love this," she muttered. "Twenty women in the room. One of them is a professional model. And all these men are telling a man how to pose for a picture in a long black dress and a lynx coat."

Billy Bishop of props pointed the wind machine at Dorothy, creating a bit of gusty winter around the splendid coat.

"Doesn't that scare you?" Sydney suggested to Dustin, since Michael might be nervous in this situation that Dorothy's auburn curls might fly away onto Madison Avenue. Dorothy did one shot with a nervous look.

Dustin changed into a kaleidoscopically colorful neo-Mandarin number with huge sleeves. The men on the set didn't think it flattered her. So Dustin changed into the Madame Blavatsky outfit with the gold sequins and the crystal ball.

Dorothy caressed the crystal ball with her ruby fingernails, lolling on the white paper floor, grinning lasciviously. The crew hooted and whistled. Sydney improvised a snake charmer's lullaby on his keyboard. Dorothy writhed . . .

Greg clicked away. Several of the men gave Dustin advice on which knee to flaunt for the sexiest recline. "Think bathing beauty," Sydney called. "1920's."

"Oh I always do," Dorothy twittered, tilting her right knee toward the camera.

"I don't believe this," Kas said

"Did you know," commented Dustin while they were re-setting, "that a woman with a breast my size is carrying two to three pounds on each side of her body? If you had to carry six pounds around on your chest all day, man, you'd feel it."

"What the mind comes up with," Sydney murmured.

Allen Weisinger touched up the recumbent Dorothy. It wasn't such an easy day for Allen. In the red-sequinned dress that made the *Tootsie* posters, Dustin had been seized with impulses—to leap; to pirouette. "Jumping and dancing, jumping and dancing," Allen said, "and the sweat gets underneath the make-up and when you go to retouch it, it just peels off." He sighed. If he appeared to be a lot thinner by now, it was probably as much from eating his heart out over sweat and whiskers and jumping and dancing as from diet.

However, everyone else was loving the "Famous Fashion Shoot." By 5:30, they had Dustin into a cowgirl outfit with a prairie skirt and a hat and a fringed vest. He had been on his feet all day; still, the fatigue hardly showed. "He looked beautiful," Owen said proudly. "It was almost like shooting commercials. He looked *beautiful*."

And it was exciting to watch that transformation, maybe more exciting for the men of *Tootsie* than the women.

Dustin's playing Dorothy was a new journey for these men and he was somehow taking it on their behalf, exploring like a scout the new terrain previously held only by the females in their lives. It wasn't just that he got to dress up in some of the most exciting clothes in New York that August, but that he could do it and come out a man, a husband father actor, a "regular" man. He could flirt and jump and dance; he could openly explore the look and feel of fear that men cannot often admit to; he could put on the raised consciousness of the actress who had been *feminized* politically; he could put it on, the way he put on the lynx coat, and still be Dustin. It was an appealing journey, every bit as mysterious and exciting as a flight on a bicycle across the moon, and when you came right down to it, every bit as far.

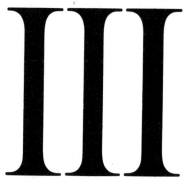**III** "IN EVERY PICTURE I'VE EVER
done," Sydney Pollack explained, "I've had to find *for myself* the
armature. It's the thing I go back to and refer to, when I look at
how to do a scene. Otherwise each scene is arbitrary and done for
and of itself.

"I don't like to discuss this with anyone else who's in the picture
because they'll say it's too intellectual. It's just for me, necessary for
me, to achieve a connection between the scenes and a sense of closure
and unity at the end.

"You have to ask yourself: what's the guideline for every scene?
So that you're playing the scene to escalate the story and store up
information and character truths."

Dramatic line is ideology to Sydney. He has to be able to see it
and say it, succinctly, and *then* he can make the movie. Thus, he
summed up the armature of *Three Days of the Condor* in a single
word: suspicion. Robert Redford, as the minor CIA intellectual who
accidentally escapes an in-house bloodbath, doesn't have suspicion
at the beginning of the movie. By the end, he will never again be
without it.

Sydney spelled out the armature of *Tootsie* as a whole movie in a simple statement of theme: a man dresses up as a woman and thereby learns to be a better man. For Sydney, that sentence was the intellectual control center of *Tootsie*. He adhered to it as the flesh adheres to the bones, and no matter what the changing writers brought him, no matter what his inventive star invented, no matter how considerations of time and money rushed the movie and pressed on Sydney (who was also producer), he never abandoned it.

The "Big Reveal Scene"—in which Dorothy Michaels rips off her disguise and reveals herself to be Michael Dorsey—both tested and proved the usefulness of the armature technique in controlling the manifold and complex factors of a film. Although the "Big Reveal" happens late in the movie, it was filmed relatively early in the shoot —when all the initial problems of make-up and script were still fresh in all minds. The throbbing heart of *Tootsie*'s final hour, the "Big Reveal" had to be exciting, a little scary, and wildly funny; and the whole movie depended on its success.

Emily Kimberly is being honored for her extraordinary service to Southwest General Hospital, and the entire staff and all the board members have gathered for a party at the home of the Board Chairman, played by a seasoned soap opera actor named Michael M. Ryan.

This segment of the soap has already been taped; but unfortunately, one of the technicians has spilled a bottle of celery tonic on it. Now the segment will have to be performed again, *live*. John Van Horn, the soap's lascivious "Dr. Brewster," is terrified because he never memorizes the inane scripts and is completely lost without the teleprompter.

But for Dorothy Michaels, the celery tonic spill has provided a golden opportunity. By now she is desperate to shed her disguise as a female. She has been proposed to by the charming Les ("the sweetest man in the whole world!" Michael Dorsey explains to his agent, George). She has almost been ravished by the elegant Van Horn. She's in love with Julie who thinks Dorothy's a lesbian. ("I love you, Dorothy," Julie has just said tearfully at her dressing room door. "But I can't love you.") She can't get out of her contract because George the agent says Dorothy is too successful. Michael's roommate Jeff speculates that there may be a morals clause in that contract so that if Dorothy did something really obscene and dis-

43

gusting . . . but no, there's nothing obscene and disgusting that hasn't already been done on the soap.

So Dorothy knows that unless she finds a way out of this mess now, she may never get to be a man again. The "Big Reveal" is her big chance.

She appears at the top of a winding staircase. She is playing Emily Kimberly, the first female character in soap opera to be "her own person." She is wearing a powder blue, tailored dress, with a Ladies Auxiliary corsage on her shoulder. She looks down at a sea of smiling people, all raising their glasses in a toast to her; "Speech, speech!" they're calling.

So she gives one.

She starts telling this story, about Anthea, daughter of Duane, who got pregnant at fifteen and contracted a disfiguring disease. . . . In the control room, Ron and Rita, director and producer, get that old sinking feeling: Dorothy is messing with the script again. "Anthea raised the little girl as her sister," Dorothy says. "Her one ambition—besides her child's happiness—was to become a nurse." The hospital staff gapes and staggers. What's she saying?! What do we do?! "The harsh realities of her beginnings had made her a champion of the underdog," Dorothy continues. This story is end-less! The director doesn't know what to tell the cameras. Dorothy is inching her way down the stairway, embroidering, unfolding. "She was shunned by the other nurses . . . she became a pariah to the doctors . . ." The cameras crash into each other. The cast is frantic. "I am not Emily Kimberly, daughter of Duane," Dorothy insists. "No, I am not! But Edward Kimberly, the recluse brother of Anthea!" And off come the eyelashes and the wig.

In front of their television sets, Sandy screams; Les drops his sandwich. In a matter of minutes, the Dorothy Michaels America loves so well has become a man! "Does Jeff know?" asks the non-plussed John Van Horn. Julie crosses the room, and despite the pleading in Michael's eyes, punches him very hard in the stomach.

To make all this happen on film was no easy task, especially be-cause it didn't just happen on film, it had to happen simultaneously on television. This meant that Sydney Pollack was directing not just one but more than six cameras, and the reactions of every single actor—on the set floor, in the control booth, on the rolling camera dollies—would have to be covered.

Dustin said there was too much material in the script for anyone to be improvising, as Michael-Dorothy was supposed to be improvising, at that moment. He didn't feel he could act the improvisation of such a big speech and be believable. Sydney said he could. Dustin was afraid that the lines didn't sound like Michael-Dorothy was making them up on the spot. Sydney said they did. Although Pollack could not by any stretch of the imagination be termed a staunch defender of text, he could get very protective of dialogue when he thought it was funny. Dustin, as with the "grits-talk" controversy, was crazy about funny lines, but he was even more concerned that they be *organic* to the character who was saying them.

It didn't help matters that Dustin was having a bad time descending those complex stairs in high heeled shoes, to which he was unaccustomed, or that his dress caught in the balustrade, or that a couple of times, he lost his balance and nearly went flying onto the floor of the set.

He and Sydney worked on the scene on Thursday and Friday. They went home for the weekend and beat on the scene with writers. Each brought back his preferred version on Monday. Then they worked on the scene again until Wednesday. Sydney acknowledged to V*ariety* that they "fought like hell about text and subtext" but never at any time was Dustin unwilling to take direction. And the direction was guided by the notion that this scene, like every scene, had an underlying armature that would lead everybody home to emotional truth.

"Here Dusty," Sydney said, "once you get this down, there's a spine to it that you've got to find and *then* you'll find the moment. Don't work on the moment. It's too early to work on the moment. What is the intention of the speech?"

"Fear," Dustin answered.

Perhaps he was thinking of Dorothy Michaels' fear that she would never get to be a man again.

"No," Sydney said. "The intention of the speech is to get even."

Perhaps he was thinking that Edward Kimberly wanted to get even with all these hospital bad guys who had killed his sister. And that Michael Dorsey wanted to get even with all those show business bad guys who had forced him into a dress in the first place.

"Yes," said Dustin. "Yes."

What Emily is really saying, Sydney said, is "I've got a trump card in my back pocket. And I'm going to tell you what it is." That motivation would work for Michael Dorsey too.

"Ladies and gentlemen," Dustin said with Dorothy's voice, "this great lady was shunned by the other ladies out of fear for their own positions."

"And the subtext of that," Sydney said, "is: Do you want to know how unjust that was? Do you want me to tell you a story that's the most unjust pathetic truth?"

"This great lady was shunned by the other nurses only out of fear for their own positions," Dustin interpreted again. "Now maybe it was the disfiguring disease . . . whatever . . . but the point is she did become a pariah to the doctors . . ."

"There's some doctors in the room," Sydney suggested. "Use them . . . the whole point is: You unjust pricks! I'm going to show you what my sister did . . ."

"But you all didn't know that she was deeply loved by her brother," Dustin continued, working the lines, "the brother who saw her pay for her . . ."

"I can't wait to see your faces when I tell you where that brother is!" Sydney said, working the intention.

"Yeah yeah," Dustin murmured.

"You know what I mean, Dusty? It needs the pleasure. It needs your own, you, Dustin's pleasure of getting even with them."

"Fill up the room with producers," Dustin suggested.

"That's the idea!" said Sydney excitedly, ready to encourage Dustin to use his personal feelings for all they were worth. "It's like telling a great story!" And he retold the story in "producer" terms. "You want to know how long we tried to make this fucking picture? And you want to know what they told us?! This won't work! That won't work! And you want to know what this picture did?! A hundred and fifty fucking million dollars! So stick it up your asses!" He hunched down toward the tense, thoughtful actor. "That's the story," he said. "It's a revenge story. Once you get the overall idea, then you can go anywhere with it."

The Pollack technique was very classical, tried and true; since Dustin came from the same theatrical culture as Sydney, he understood it perfectly. As Michael Dorsey, teaching acting to a classful of kids at the beginning of *Tootsie*, he uses the same technique.

"Be specific," he says. The idea was that if the actor approached every single event in the story with a *specific objective* firmly in mind, then you could have television cameras crashing into each other and tales unfolding and characters within characters within characters revealing themselves, and the scene would never run off its moorings.

Sydney and Dustin also shared a common definition of good comic acting, based on the *Candid Camera* example. "I was always a fan of *Candid Camera*," Dustin had told *Playboy*, "because it caught human beings in wonderfully farcical, absurd kinds of behavior." When Sydney directed the crowd at the base of the staircase in the "Big Reveal" scene, he asked: "Do any of you remember that one *Candid Camera* where somebody goes to mail a letter and there's a voice in the mailbox? Yes? Okay. What's funny? The voice in the mailbox or the person's reaction? . . . We *think* the absurdity is the voice; but that's not what makes us laugh. What makes us laugh is the person who doesn't expect the voice to come out of the mailbox and absolutely freezes and doesn't know what to do."

Emily Kimberly's story was to be the unexpected voice in the mailbox. And Sydney wanted the crowd of soap opera actors to react with the same innocence and lack of self-awareness that made the reaction of the person on *Candid Camera* so reliably funny.

"Now all of a sudden," Sydney told the group, "Dustin departs from the text. And that starts the minute he begins walking down the stairs. Now without doing it by rote—it would take you a second to let it seep in so I don't want everybody to turn the minute he starts to walk—what I need to see you do, *quietly*, don't *show* me anything, just do it for yourselves, is begin to say: What the hell is going on?

"First you begin to wonder.

"Then you would maybe begin to try to get some signal from somebody around you.

"And then what I would try to get you to do if you can . . . is begin to get lost in his story, and begin to start listening. Pretty soon it starts to be a pretty good story . . . somebody with a disfiguring disease, and somebody coming to a hospital . . . so you just kind of let yourself react the way you would react. Don't think of it as being for a camera. Just do it for yourself. *If you do it for yourself, I'll see it*. Don't *show* me anything. All right? Let's try it."

Sydney's search for bedrock, for a synoptic clarity that would make it impossible for people to do what he didn't want them to do, pervaded his work on *Tootsie*, extending far beyond the script into every aspect of the filming and the producing.

"He's terribly efficient," Michael M. Ryan said after working with him on the "Big Reveal." "He has solved so many problems in advance that when he gets to the set, he can improvise if he wants to."

Thus, during the "Big Reveal," Sydney chopped out a couple of Ryan's lines right on the spot. It may have disappointed the actor, who only had a few lines to begin with, but he had to agree, it made things "cleaner." These on-the-spot inspirations happened again and again: let's try this camera angle we hadn't thought of before; let's solve the space problem in this tight bathroom with this lens, that technique. And just in case, after all the takes, someone still had something they wanted to try which might yield some small glory heretofore unimagined, *Tootsie* had a system of "freebies." These were extra shots in which the untried could be tried. (Dustin had worked this way before, on *Kramer vs Kramer.*) The cast got "freebies" and once in a while, so did Owen Roizman. They tended to be slightly wild; often useless; sometimes priceless. They were a sort of "interest" that the movie collected because Sydney had invested so heavily in his "homework."

While so many creative people suffer endlessly because of their powerlessness to control the technologies in which they must work, or to manage the money that ultimately manages them, Sydney is one of the very few who seems to have mastered it all. A playwright once urged a seminar of prospective dramatists to study acting. "If you don't know what they do," she cautioned, "they'll do it to you." Sydney Pollack operated with the same suspicious aforethought.

Thus, as a young actor he had plunged out of the theatre and into the very different craft of television acting. He appeared in several Hemingway adaptations directed by John Frankenheimer. Frankenheimer brought him to Hollywood as a dialogue coach on *The Young Savages* starring Burt Lancaster. Both Frankenheimer and Lancaster urged him to start directing. In the late '50s and early '60s, Sydney directed more than 80 television shows, mastering the cameras, the time frames, the video techniques in such shows as *The Defenders, Naked City, Ben Casey* and *Chrysler Theatre*. He won an Emmy in

1965 for *The Game*, and in the same year, directed his first feature film, *The Slender Thread*. He received an Academy Award nomination for *They Shoot Horses, Don't They?* But his great reputation had been as a director of actors. He launched Jane Fonda as a dramatic actress in *They Shoot Horses*. He did the same for Barbra Streisand in *The Way We Were*. His abiding association with Robert Redford started with *This Property Is Condemned* in 1966 and continued through four subsequent films. (They met when Sydney and Redford acted together in a film called *The War Hunt* in 1962.)

"I don't think of myself as an innovator at all," Pollack told *Esquire* during the filming of *Absence of Malice*. "What I like to do is take the form of traditional, classical movies and see how much I can get away with without changing the form. I gave up on visual tricks a long time ago. I don't think I do them well."

Sydney told Rocky Lang that he knew he would never be "a Fellini or a Bergman." He behaved like a man who had no pretensions to the history of all time, and seemed to take pride in accepting his own limitations. But maybe that was just for the record. Because on the set of *Tootsie*, at least, Sydney Pollack seemed determined not to be limited by not knowing something. He could do everything on the movie. Everything.

"I've seen him paint sets and take apart microphones," David McGiffert testified. "He at all times has an overall schematic in his head. And knows where he is within that schematic at all times. That's an unusual quality . . . for film, because it's made up entirely of bits and pieces. So to know not only what should happen with the bit, the piece, the scene, but how that works in relation to other scenes, what has happened before and after, and how to modulate all that and make a film is an unusual quality and Sydney has that quality. He knows the pitfalls that a production company can get into. And so he's able to help other people in their jobs because he understands what their job is about.

"And sometimes he can do their job.

"He's very gifted mentally. I mean the man . . . is . . . bright."

This Renaissance persona of Sydney's could occasionally ruffle the artisans on the set, especially if they thought *they* knew it all. Sydney admitted to *American Film* that he had fought with James Wong

Howe on the set of *This Property Is Condemned*: "He was right that there is no point in hiring James Wong Howe and then telling him what to do," Sydney said. "But you must find a way to communicate enough information so that you get what you want, and leave him room to create. And there is always room, because I'll never know as much as a cameraman knows. However, I certainly want to know what happens with perspective, what happens with f/stop changes, and what happens with intercutting from one lens to another."

His extraordinary close working relationship with Owen Roizman came from a mutual acceptance of style. The unflappable Roizman would slide off the camera dolly so Sydney could sit in his chair. But even Owen had had his moments of artistic rebellion against Sydney's overwhelming need to know everything.

"On *Condor*," Owen said, "Sydney had just come from Japan from shooting *Yakuza*. And he never trusted the guys out there reading meters. So he used to read the meter all the time, and he checked the contrasts in his viewing glass the same as the cameraman would do.

"And when I saw this for the first time, I said: 'What's this?' Because I have never had a director take meter readings on the set before.

"So I started kidding around with him.

"I would take the meter out and read the light. I worked at very low light levels then, and he wasn't used to that, and I'd tell the assistant cameraman what f/stop I was using and I'd give him an f/stop that was totally unbelievable for the amount of light that was on the set. And Sydney would say: 'How can you see at that f/stop?' And I said: 'Don't worry, Syd, I have a special way of doing it, it'll be fine.' And just before we'd go, the assistant cameraman would open up the f/stop we were *really* gonna use.

"And we'd go to dailies and, of course, the stuff looked fine."

Owen no longer reacted to Sydney's expertise with the resentment that might have characterized younger egos; he knew the light meter was still around Sydney's neck, ready for use at any time. "Sydney's had a lot of experience with technical things," Owen said. "And he's very inquisitive. So when something technical comes along, he wants to find out about it." These were the facts of life. Sydney was a rampaging autodidact. He had none of the learning neuroses that plagued the formally educated. He could do art and he could do technology. You could teach him anything; therefore, you couldn't tell him much.

"Even though he needs us," David said, "he doesn't need us to the degree that most filmmakers do."

But who does he lean on?

"It's a good question."

What makes him crazy?

"Incompetence."

Of course, people who want to control everything generally spend their lives looking for something they can't control so their lives will be more interesting. The harder the job, the more fun they have.

Except that Sydney Pollack would swear to you that he was not having fun. "If you think waking up every morning with a $20 million monkey on your back is fun," he told *Variety*, "you're wrong." No, he insisted, what he was having was not fun but *fear*. "When I was a kid and I would go to the park and get on the roller coaster," he said, "the minute it would start, I realized I had made a terrible mistake and I'd say 'No! No! I want to get off!' But it was too late already. Scary. Films always feel like that to me. I want to say: 'Wait! Wait! Wait!' "

But there was no time to wait; to think; "no time to do the *dramatic* work," Sydney said, knitting his mobile face in frustration.

Dustin shared this anxiety. Wait,! he would say in the morning. Wait, let's discuss this; rehearse this. Although some film actors deliberately spurn more than cursory rehearsal, the better to preserve spontaneity (Redford is one of those, Sydney said), Dustin wanted rehearsal badly, precisely because there was no "locked-in" script to lie like foam under the picture and cushion the ride.

"But Sydney isn't a big rehearsal man," explained Ron Schwary. "And if Sydney had wanted to rehearse for a month, say, before the shoot began, he couldn't have because the actors weren't cast. Jessica's deal wasn't set until right before she came on. Bill Murray wasn't cast until very late. But Dustin wanted rehearsal. Because Dustin is from the theatre." (Schwary pronounces it "thee-aitre.")

Certainly Dustin wasn't the first actor in Sydney's life to require more rehearsal than Sydney thought he had time for. Al Pacino, a theatre-trained actor, had made the same demands on *Bobby Deerfield*. But if Dustin wanted rehearsal, it wasn't just because he was *from* the theatre. It was because he was playing Michael Dorsey, an actor in the theatre, and in doing that, he was feeling Michael Dorsey's need.

"Lookit, it's an empiric thing," Sydney offered. "If somebody says to you they get more comfortable with rehearsal, then you can't argue that. But you can say to them, I wish I could convince you to be confident without rehearsal, because when you haven't rehearsed, there's something else that's there." Sydney was relaxed when he said this. It was late in the shoot; the debate days of July were long past. "When you're rehearsing in the theatre, you're weaning them [the actors] from dependence on you. Your subtext in your work as a director is: You don't need me. Because when the curtain goes up, I won't be there.

"It is exactly the opposite in film. In film, they only have to understand it enough to be able to do it right once while the camera is rolling. So in film, you want them to be somewhat more dependent on you. Because the only one who is ever really gonna be alone is you, the director, when you're putting it all together. And you can't look at it in the cutting room and yell 'Goddammit, you were wrong!' because they're gone, gone on another picture.

"If I'm the one who's gonna be alone pulling together all the pieces, I have to make sure I've got the right pieces."

What worried Dustin was that the pieces Sydney would have in the end would not be the pieces he, Dustin, would have provided if only he had had more rehearsal (as in the theatre); more *independence* (as in the theatre) within the script; over the script; from the director.

"Every actor doesn't really want to be an actor, I don't think," Dustin explained. "Every actor doesn't really want to be the interpreter. What we'd really like to be is the creator. You don't want to have to do what somebody else wrote. That's all right when you're doing a play because you have control over your performance. But in a movie, you don't know what *they're* gonna do with it!" His thin face darkened. His eyes glittered with stored-up fires. "You don't know how they're gonna cut it! They can destroy you! They can destroy your concept of it! *Very easily!*"

Dustin's "they" stood for producers and directors.

He had tried to achieve the feminization of Ted Kramer in the filming, he said, "when they would let me in the cutting room. . . ."

"I did *Alfredo* because they told me I could do it in Italian," he had said to *Playboy*. "But they lied to me and I had to do it in English."

Dustin didn't invent the hostile "they," and nobody knew that better than Sydney, for he had been an actor, he had been helpless, he had spent twenty years learning all the things you needed to know so you wouldn't be a helpless actor. The "freebies" were one technique of allaying Dustin's fear. He always got to try it at least once his way. Sydney estimated that one in five of Dustin's "freebies" yielded "something we can use in the picture."

The same ratio apparently applied to a rehearsal which Dustin wanted and Jessica Lange wanted, and which Sydney took time out to do midway through the morning make-up hour.

The scene they were rehearsing shall be called the "Lesbian Scene." Actually, there are no lesbians in *Tootsie*. But at one point, Michael is so overcome with passion for Julie that he forgets he is supposed to be a woman and almost kisses Julie, thereby convincing Julie that Dorothy's a lesbian and giving Julie some second thoughts about herself too.

The scene takes place in the mauve, pink and baby blue apartment that Peter Larkin had conceived for a national soap opera star who is herself as delectable as a piece of candy. Ruth Morley, who called Julie's wardrobe style "sophisticated rural," put the actress in suede several times during the film and for this scene supplied bubble gum pink suede pants to go with the apartment. Dustin, you could be sure, was set to play the "Lesbian Scene" for every laugh it might yield.

Jessica Lange, unlike Teri Garr, was not automatically cast in comedies. Her fascination as a screen personality came from the sex appeal that Sydney and many other men had spotted in *King Kong*. It wasn't the pulchritudinous kind associated with Monroe, Taylor, Loren and Welch that women too enjoy, but a kind of laid-back, slowed-down, cooled-out sexiness that appeals *particularly* to men. "Jessica's got what Redford's got. Presence," commented Dustin.

The *Tootsie* women admired Jessica though because she fought for her terms and won; because she absented herself, cool, polite, and professional, from the artistic disputes that embroiled Sydney and Dustin; because she whooped and tumbled with her friendly little daughter in the dressing room, not at all a laid-back parent.

However, Sydney seemed to be doing everything he could in *Tootsie* to deepen the impression of Jessica as a cool, languorous enigma who, like Botticelli's Venus on the half shell, was either waking up after a long submergence or getting ready to turn in again. Thus, one of Julie's most memorable scenes takes place while she is falling asleep in the same bed as Dorothy. She occasionally comforts herself with a glass of wine—or two, or three—so that even when she is upset, she is slowed-down and tipsy. If she rides a horse, or cooks a meal in a farm kitchen, she does it in what Sydney called "just the right amount of slow motion." So intent was the film on Jessica's style and appeal that the designers actually hit scientific paydirt. In the *New York Times* Science section the following August, it was revealed that bubble-gum pink was the preferred color of rooms used to calm manic children.

For the "Lesbian Scene," Jessica strolled onto the rehearsal set in pale dungarees and sweater. The hair stylist had put some dripping solution on her blonde locks, but she still looked terrific, and listened gravely while Sydney mapped out her blocking.

The "Lesbian Scene" was to take place on the plum colored sofa. Dustin and Jessica were to do their girl talk/confidante conversation (Julie has just broken up with Ron and wonders unhappily whom she's going to have dinner with from now on) and then in an unguarded moment, they forget themselves and begin their kiss. It would actually happen except that Julie aborts it at the last moment by leaping up off the sofa. Suddenly the phone rings. It's Les, Julie's father, who's in love with Dorothy. The distraught Julie puts her hand over the receiver and says to the distraught Dorothy, "You've got to tell him!"

"Tell him what?!" says Dorothy.

Julie does *not* say, "Tell him that you're a lesbian," but clearly that's what she's implying.

Rehearsal.

The two female faces approached each other for the unplanned kiss.

Jessica leapt up.

Dustin tipped over and plunged face forward into the plush pillows.

Sydney laughed, but he didn't really want that.

Dustin suggested that another way might be to let the kiss happen, sort of friendly at first.

"Here's the only thought I have," he said, "and if it's no good, throw it out. But if she [Julie] is upset and I'm . . . Dorothy's comforting her, here's my thought . . . the first time I kiss . . . it's just a thought . . . in other words, I was thinking if I could start . . . it may be no good, if you don't like it, I don't care, but if I start kissing her to comfort her, the longer she misunderstands it, maybe, the better . . ."

And he began kissing Jessica lightly, little kisses on her face, getting progressively hotter.

Jessica didn't think she would misunderstand that for very long.

"It's dangerous," Sydney said, "and it's not clean. If you guys can just look at each other for a moment and then you can just begin to move toward her . . . that's clean, and it'll be clear." He turned to Jessica, to see her reaction. "When somebody makes a mistaken pass at you . . . I'm sure everybody's had this . . . you feel bad for them . . ."

"A woman's never made a pass at me," Jessica said.

"Oh you poor thing!" Sydney cried. "We'll have to fix that!"

And they rehearsed some more.

Dustin and Jessica conspired, making Sydney stand off at a distance, so they could cook up a surprise.

When the phone rang, Jessica, who was supposed to grab the phone, didn't grab the phone, she grabbed a ceramic corn cob and yelled "Hello!" into its kernels.

Sydney laughed . . . but you never knew when Sydney laughed whether he was going to keep it in the movie.

During the next rehearsal, she answered the corn cob and *then* the phone and said, "Oh, hi Ron." (Ron is the soap director whom Julie has just dumped.)

Sydney laughed.

Clearly, he didn't want that at all.

Dustin suggested they put in a spin-off of an old Mel Brooks joke, the punchline of which was approximately, "I'm not a lesbian, I'm a thespian!" He gave up right away on that one. However, the inspired moment when Jessica answered the ceramic corn cob instead of the phone remained in the final version of the movie. The actors were hitting just as Sydney had figured, one for five.

. . .

The "Late for Dinner Scene" didn't require as much rehearsal as the "Lesbian Scene" because it was short, and tight, with simple, small actions and comic lines that snapped with a precise impact. Unlike almost kissing another woman, being late for dinner didn't lend itself to a variety of approaches. Besides, who had the strength? It was over 90 degrees in New York and a lot hotter in the serpentine apartment on 100th and Riverside where they were shooting. Cables pumping power for the air conditioning and the lights snaked from the trucks outside up through the old corridors. The old building seemed to be groaning and creaking in protest.

The apartment belonged to Sandy Lester (played by Teri Garr), an out-of-work actress who favored dizzy printed antique clothes dug from bins on Sixth Avenue. She had been Michael Dorsey's friend and student for many years. Now all of a sudden, she was his lover too.

The dizzy prints had been picked by Ruth Morley to augment the dizzy confusion of Sandy, who has none of the attributes that Sydney Pollack and Dustin Hoffman ascribe to a mature woman. Sandy doesn't have children. Sandy doesn't fight for what she wants. Sandy forgives you so fast when you do something bad to her that it is impossible to take her seriously. Besides, Sandy comes from California, the Never Never Land of eternal youth. In a scene that Teri Garr improvised on the set, she gets locked in the bathroom at Michael's surprise party and nobody even notices that she's gone. Of course, she never cooks. Which is why it is so hugely important that she has invited Michael to dinner and prepared a meat loaf.

All of this was created in deliberate contrast with Julie, Michael's true love. Though blonde and beautiful, just like Sandy, Julie comes from a farm in upstate New York, with real cows, real manure, and a large kitchen in which she cooks a hearty dinner with loads of side dishes for her father and her friend Dorothy. Julie's pace was completely different from Sandy's. Julie achieved a lot slowly; Sandy achieved nothing fast.

Teri Garr's career had been built on movie comedy. She had appeared in another Gelbart film—*Oh, God!*—in which George Burns played God and Teri played a housewife. She had been funny in

Young Frankenstein, daffy in *The Black Stallion*, confused in *Close Encounters of the Third Kind* and was supposed to be all three as Sandy in *Tootsie*.

Teri's background was theatrical. She had been a chorus-line dancer. She had been to the O'Neill Playwrights Festival, where experienced actors who care about original drama lend themselves indiscriminately to new scripts. Long hours. Bad pay. Great fun. "I'd go back in a minute," Teri said.

So when it came to the "Late for Dinner Scene," Sydney Pollack was dealing with two actors who had enormous experience in *theatrical* comedy, and who could be counted on to cook up between themselves all kinds of reliable schtick and classical timing.

When Sandy Lester prepares the meat loaf dinner for Michael Dorsey, she gets herself and her tiny dining table all spiffy, and waits.

Michael is late. The meat loaf is burning. The wine is going flat. Michael is very late. The meat loaf has burned. The wine has been drunk—by Sandy. Michael is *three hours late!*

When he finally arrives, still wet from a recent shower, Sandy greets him with the heavy-lidded "I've heard this shit before" expression for which Teri Garr became famous on the set of *Tootsie*.

Michael gives her a long explanation for his lateness. Sandy with self-hating suspicion tells him that she went over to his apartment when he didn't show up for dinner, and she saw with her own eyes "that fat woman" entering his building.

The "fat woman" is, of course, Dorothy Michaels making a quick change back into Michael Dorsey who had suddenly remembered his dinner date with Sandy.

Michael declares that the woman is a typist friend of Jeff's who comes to help him with his play and can do 100 words a minute. And besides, he has brought Sandy her favorite flavor of ice cream, chocolate chocolate chip.

(Julie has no food weaknesses. Sandy can be bought, had, quieted, neutralized with chocolate.)

So Sandy believes Michael's lies.

She apologizes for making trouble.

She nibbles on the chocolate chocolate chip.

"Did you see 'that cow' they cast in the soap instead of me?" she says chattily to the man who is playing "the cow" in question.

"What cow?" Dustin answers.

57

The "Late for Dinner Scene" couldn't miss—but it wasn't going well. It was Monday. The heat and the discomfort of the location were getting to everybody; even McGiffert seemed on the verge of not saying "Please" or "Thank you," although to his everlasting credit, this never happened. Sydney looked overburned from his weekend. His entreaties to the actors, usually so animated and punchy, seemed automatic; uninspired.

Dustin, on the other hand, was set to go. Energy radiated from his small frame, hotter than the heat. Dustin and Teri had rehearsed in her trailer before the shoot. Dustin had started with his script, she without hers.

"She's supposed to be the head of the hospital, supposed to be tough!" said Teri of the actress who landed the role of Emily Kimberly. "She's not tough. She's a wimp! . . . I think I'm gonna say 'wimp,' Dustin."

"Sissy Mary," he suggested. "Puffball."

"Lightweight. Flimsy. Transparent," she counter-suggested.

"I like puffball. Let's start over."

They did it over. And over. They did it in the rickety elevator that took them up to the set floor.

"I love working with Teri Garr," Dustin said. "We have the same comic rhythm. The same comic instincts, and I like her too. We should be married. No. We should be divorced and working together." (Like the light opera stars of Kiss Me Kate. Something about Teri suggests musical comedy to many people.)

In the apartment, the crew was spilling water on the floor to mask the squeaking of the camera dolly wheels. Dustin began nibbling on the salad from Sandy's dinner table, until someone worried about matching shots stopped him. He and Teri tried the scene again.

"I saw that 'fat woman' go into your apartment," Sandy says.

"Oh, she's Jeff's typist," Michael explains. He pauses; what Sandy has just said sinks in. Trying to conceal his concern, he says: "You think she's fat?"

It wasn't quite right.

Dustin started over.

Sandy opens the door, gives him that "I've heard this shit before" look. He inches past the door, which is half closed like Teri's large light eyes.

"Listen Sandy," he blathers nervously. "I was shampooing my hair and the shower went off and I got shampoo in my eyes and I couldn't see and I slipped on a bar of soap and I had to go to five different stores to get your favorite kind of ice cream, chocolate chocolate chip."

Dustin did it again. And again. The laughs he and Teri had given themselves on the rickety elevator evaporated in the repetition. The floorboards had to be wet down again. Teri's shoes were making noise too. Props took them away for an anti-squeak waxing. Dustin paced, annoyed with himself. He was losing his energy. The twinkling Teri, usually lightning fast as Tinker Bell, was growing blue and thoughtful.

The comedy was in "the beats," the counted pause before the line. Dustin and Sydney and Teri, the writers, *all* the writers knew that. When Jack Benny got laughs, it wasn't because of what he said or how he said it but *when* he said it. Timing was the ultimate guarantor of the comic payoff. "Women should be beaten regularly," says Elliot dashingly in *Private Lives*, "like gongs." But if he doesn't say it with the right one-two before "like gongs," even Noel Coward won't get the laugh. Sydney said that Mel Brooks said that people who couldn't do music couldn't do comedy, which was why he might feel confident of Dustin who had trained as a concert pianist and Teri who had been in two ballet companies by the time she was seventeen. But today, on Riverside Drive, the beats weren't working. And you didn't have to be a musician to see that they weren't working because the *timing* was off.

Sydney summoned back his strength and his words. He massaged Teri's slender arms, talking. He paced alongside Dustin, just a little, talking. As much as Dustin might appear to need comfort on this trying movie, he certainly didn't need stroking; in fact, it would have insulted him. The catch-22 in the collaborative theatrical arts is that directors get hired because they're so good at manipulating people, but by virtue of the fact that they're always being manipulated, actors—and writers—often develop a violent sensitivity in this area, and so the best directors learn to get what they want without obvious condescension. Thus, Sydney forebore, waiting for the actors to find their music.

On the next take, to give them a new lift-off, he vamped the pretext of the scene, suggesting but not mandating the scene's *intention* to Teri.

"There he is, that bum," he said, "he's kept you waiting three hours. What kind of excuse is he gonna have now? Okay. Action." They did it again.

"Save it. One more time. Getting close, guys, that's very good." If only they could time out the scene's funniest line—"You think she's fat?"—everything else might fall into place.

"I'm gonna get it now," Dustin growled. He approached the door like it was his sparring partner. "Okay, I've got it."

But Teri misjudged the timing and cut a line.

"You can't interrupt 'fat woman,' honey," Sydney said, "otherwise the whole scene doesn't work."

The more Teri and Dustin nibbled on the chocolate chocolate chip, the more syllables they added to the script. It was as though the ice cream was going into the lines instead of into the actors, who remained thin while the scene got so fat it couldn't move.

"It's funnier to say 'Cow?' than 'What cow?', Dusty," Sydney offered.

Teri and Dustin grabbed angrily at their pages. When *Tootsie* people started looking at the *script*, you *knew* they must be feeling rocky. Dustin dealt with the crisis by Groucho Marxing Teri.

"You're supposed to be the straight man here, sweetheart," he interjected with wagging eyebrows and narrow eyes. "Don't try to get a series out of this."

She laughed; the lights went on again in Tinker Bell. The scene worked. The company, tired and grouchy and glad it was over, piled into the groaning, creaking elevator and headed down to a nice cold lunch.

However, the elevator finally rebelled and got stuck between floors. Tod Maitland, who worked the sound boom, managed to climb out and guide the old machine to ground level. Sydney kept everybody calm until they were safe.

Making *Tootsie* happen . . .

Director Sydney Pollack with Owen Roizman, Director of Photography.

Ruth Morley, Costume
Designer (left), with
Jennifer Nichols of
wardrobe.

Hoffman, Pollack, and
Renee Bodner, Script
Supervisor on location on
New York's West 18th
Street.

Pollack and David McGiffert, First Assistant Director.

Hoffman resting off-camera with Bill Murray.

Bill Murray, Dorothy Pearl, Make-Up Artist, and Hoffman. Behind Dorothy Pearl is Ann Guerin, Unit Publicist.

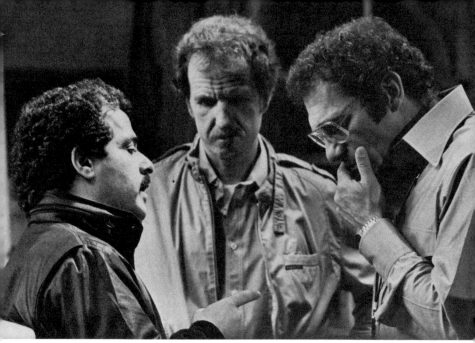

Ron Schwary, left, with Jerry Molen of Production, and Pollack.

Pollack and baby Amy Lawrence in a relaxed moment between takes.

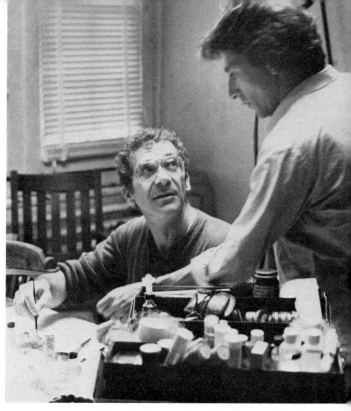

Hoffman and Pollack discuss Michael's make-up.

Michael teaches an acting class.

Hoffman and Teri Garr in the "Soap Opera Audition Scene."

Hoffman and Pollack consult . . . and perform.

The "Tomato Scene." Michael
confronts his agent, played by a
despairing Sydney Pollack, who
pulls no punches. "No one will
hire you," he shouts. Michael
responds, "Oh, yeah?"

Dustin Hoffman becomes Dorothy Michaels . . .

Pollack and Allen
Weisinger check on
Dorothy's make-up and
hair.

Hoffman is dressed as Dorothy by Jennifer Nichols and Franke Piazza.

Off-camera, at Dorothy's closet.

Dorothy's character is constantly reviewed by Hoffman and Pollack.

Jessica Lange plays Julie Nichols.

Jessica with Dabney Coleman (above) and Amy Lawrence (below).

Teri Garr plays Sandy Lester.

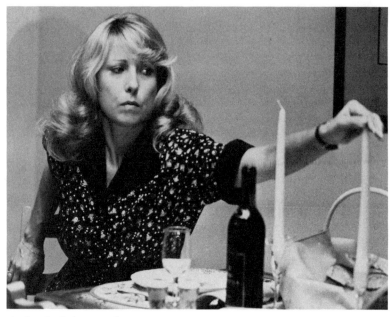

As Sandy, being stood up.

As Sandy, exploding.

Dorothy deals with sex . . . and love . . .

With Jessica Lange in the important "Girl Talk Scene."

Off-camera, with wife, Lisa Hoffman.

With Geena Davis, who plays April, the soap's radiologist, in the backstage ladies' dressing room.

With Charles Durning, as Les, up at the farm.

With Jessica.

With Amy.

Dorothy with her producer,
played by Doris Belack.

Dorothy with her soap co-star,
played by George Gaynes.

Dorothy with her agent, played by Pollack, in the famous "Russian Tea Room Scene" (above) and, later, on West 57th Street (below).

Dorothy signs autographs while Julie and her father look on.

Preparing for the "Big Reveal Scene." Hoffman makes a point to Pollack.

Allen Weisinger touches up Hoffman's make-up.

Pollack demonstrates how to take a punch.

Jessica Lange delivers it.

IN THE EARLY '60S, WHEN Dustin Hoffman was looking for work in the theatre, he was one of thousands of unemployed actors who clung onto the nether reaches of New York City's economy, ready to take marginal jobs at marginal wages until the world should discover their greatness.

Nothing much had changed by the time he returned to New York to play Michael Dorsey in *Tootsie*. Ellen Burstyn, the President of Actors' Equity, estimated that hers was surely the only union that *expected* 80% unemployment among its members at any given time. "There's one big difference between Michael and Dorothy," Dustin said. "Michael's unemployed. And Dorothy's working. I mean *Dorothy's working*. DOROTHY'S WORKING! If you understand that, then the movie works. Because that's what being an actor is. It's the state of being unemployed."

What keeps these *luftmenschen* going? What keeps them dressing for auditions, paying for classes in voice, in dance, in fencing, sending out pictures and resumes and hoping for, no, *counting on* success? It isn't just the traditional American need to be rich and famous. It's a need for love. To be loved by the people. To show the people how much you care about them. To show how much you *are* them.

Since many actors have to feed this passion on a diet of rejection, they sometimes begin to harbor the potential for violent anger inside themselves, as many spurned lovers do.

"I had the feeling on *Straight Time*," Dustin said, "that there was a correlation between actors and people in prison." (*Straight Time* was a film about a man who has been in jail so much he can't make it on the outside any more.) "People in prison are not always dumb people. I mean, they're very perceptive, some of them, very bright, and you could almost use the word 'gifted.'

"But for happenstance, circumstance, whatever, they got busted. They could have been a gifted this, that or the other, but they got a shitty run right from the gate and I always felt *that's what promotes violence*. All my friends . . . Gene Hackman, Bobby Duvall, we couldn't get *arrested*. That's the term we used funnily enough, we couldn't get a job . . . It's the inability to generate for yourself the creative impulse *and to cook it*! If you can't do that, you go out and hit somebody!"

Dustin, a Californian by birth, had met Hackman while they were both acting students at the Pasadena Playhouse. Dustin's father was at one time a set decorator and a great fan of comedy. His mother, Lillian, had named Dustin's brother Ronald (now a government economist) for Ronald Colman and Dustin for a cowboy of the silent screen, Dustin Farnum. Eager for theatrical action, Dustin and Gene Hackman had gone to New York together in 1958.

"I spent two years in Strasberg's class," Dustin recalled. "I wasn't one of his 'followers,' but he was great to listen to. I always thought it was terrible the way they'd follow him around like he was God and could make them be Jimmy Dean or Marlon Brando. I hung around with Gene and Bobby Duvall. Bobby . . . studied with Meisner. Hackman studied with George Morrison."

The adventures of Hackman, Duvall and Hoffman back in those cold, dark days became the stuff of hilarious oral history between takes at *Tootsie*. But it was the *rejection*, the unemployment, the waiting and waiting and waiting to be discovered and loved, that bore on Michael Dorsey's character. So that was what Dusty was remembering.

"I never earned more than $3000 a year before I was thirty-one years old," he once told the *Ladies' Home Journal*. "If my parents hadn't sent me money every week, I couldn't have survived."

He worked behind a counter at Macy's, pulling Candid Camera-type stunts on the customers. Once he accused an innocent woman of shop lifting just to see the expression on her face. He did telephone solicitation for charity. He strung Hawaiian orchids together to make leis in the flower district. He helped to reorganize the research morgue at *Time*. He got a job in a psychiatric institute and actually aided in holding down patients who were undergoing electric shock therapy. He worked as a waiter and a dishwasher in a multitude of eating places, enlivening the hours by practicing his French accent on the customers. He drove a taxi. He taught drama to dead end kids in the Bronx and enthusiastic amateurs in New Jersey. He demonstrated toys at Christmas. Once he almost managed to sell somebody Gene Hackman's little boy, pitching him as an extremely lifelike doll, just to hear how the poor customer screamed when she touched the warm human flesh. He typed for the Yellow Pages. He looked so poor and scruffy that a fellow actor said "Jeez, you're never gonna get work unless you look right!" So when Dustin finally got a part on *Naked City* and earned $500, he spent $150 of it on a new coat. "When I tried it on," he told *Playboy*'s Dick Meryman, "I was literally sweating. I had never spent so much money on myself before . . . I went to pay for it and I was trembling. Such luxury! When I walked out with the coat . . . everything went black in front of me . . . And I thought—I really did —'I'm being punished.' What it was was the night of the big blackout."

This incident with the coat was one of Dustin's last encounters with the neuroses of poverty before *The Graduate* came and took it all away forever. Playing Michael Dorsey was, therefore, a colossal effort to retrieve those neuroses, all of them: the anger about rejection; the mixed feelings of camaraderie and jealousy toward other actors; the intense knowledge that you had nothing to lose because you had nothing so why not pull a stunt for your own entertainment? On a hapless customer in the toy department. Or a patron in a restaurant. Or on a big, powerful, silly soap opera and a big, powerful, self-satisfied agent.

The agent in *Tootsie*, George Fields, had his office in the Columbia Pictures Building on Fifth Avenue. It was to this lovely building that the *Tootsie* crew came with its snaking cables full of power to set up the "Tomato Scene." George Fields was being played by Sydney Pollack.

The *Tootsie* crew turned the tenth floor into the offices of C.A.A. —Creative Artists Agency—a *real* show business agency of which Michael Ovitz, Dustin's agent *and* Sydney's agent, is a major selling feature. Masking went up over the office fluorescents. Extras roamed the narrow hallways, indistinguishable from the regular employees. Rocky Lang was there with his documentary crew. Ann Guerin, the soft-spoken unit publicist of *Tootsie*, arrived with the French press in tow: a sweet young girl from *Figaro* accompanied by a photographer. The space grew tighter and tighter as the Columbia Pictures clerks and secretaries pressed in toward the movie-making with a determined crush, trying to catch a glimpse, a whiff of what it was all about.

Despite their Columbia working address, they were about as familiar with movie-making as a Food Stamps official is with cattle ranching. Production assistants like Kato Wittich, Justin Cooke, and Tom Burns pressed everybody back with polite imprecations, never shouting but increasingly troubled. These Columbia people spent their daily work lives under huge posters advertising the success of Dustin Hoffman's films—in Cannes; in Munich; in London —and it was finally their turn. Joe Reidy, the second AD, a wise young man from Ohio, asked them to move back. David McGiffert asked them to move back. But they turned cold eyes on the repeated requests and did not move back.

The lighting crew rewalled the lobby with white styrofoam. The young actress who was playing a C.A.A. receptionist took her seat at the front desk. Dustin would soon burst out of the elevator and rush past her to accost his agent George.

The space was very tight. The crowd, friendly but inexorable, lapped up against the heels of Sydney's cowboy boots.

"Quiet please," David said.

"Now reach for the phone, dear," Sydney told the actress at the reception desk.

"Mary," she said nicely.

"Reach for the phone, Mary," Syd said, also nicely.

"Please stop talking, folks," David said. "That's how it gets quiet."

Dustin, as Michael, was wearing his usual blue sweatshirt, and a jacket just like the one he had bought at Modell's Army/Navy store when he himself was an out-of-work actor, long before the $150 coat days. He made friends with the extras. He made friends with Mary Donnet, who had a line or two as the startled receptionist. Just when it finally got quiet, the elevator opened and someone in it called out: "Need a leading lady?"

On the third rehearsal, Sydney added a coffee cup and a crossword puzzle to the receptionist's desk, undoubtedly a touch inspired by his ebullient secretary Carrie who was a crossword zealot of certifiable extremes. "Picture coming up," he said finally, and the hairdressing and make-up people surged over Hoffman like a wave. He burst out of the elevator. They did a take.

Michael's motivation for bursting out of the elevator was supposed to be fury. He had just found out that an old actor friend of his had been sent by George Fields to audition for Eugene O'Neill's *The Iceman Cometh*, and had actually gotten the part, a part which Michael Dorsey knew he could do better and for which he had not even been suggested to read! Fury! Outrage! Jealousy!

"When you come out of the elevator, Dusty," Sydney said, "be a little more out of breath."

"More?" Dustin asked.

"Little more," Sydney answered.

On the next take, Dustin was *panting* as he rushed into the lobby. But he didn't quite hit the right spot under the light for the best shot. It was a hard spot to hit because the floor was in the picture and thus unmarkable. They did another take. The crowd of onlookers, which like all uninitiated crowds was beginning to be astounded at how *boring* movie-making actually was, shuffled and talked and shifted. "Please folks, if you're gonna watch, please don't let me hear you," Sydney said. "We're working with live sound here."

They did another take. Dustin was so out of breath that it was logical to assume he had run all the way down Fifth Avenue to get to this lobby.

David's headset died. He borrowed Kato's. They did another take. It was perfect. "Okay, this is a freebie," Sydney called. Dustin barrelled out of the elevator, right into a stray clerk.

"Oh, excuse me," she said.

"Excuse *me*," he answered.

"Oh my God!" she cried, realizing who he was, what *this* must be. If only she had kept her innocence, Sydney Pollack might have saved it.

Michael runs past George's secretary, into George's office. George is on the phone. "I'm talking to the Coast," George says.

"New York is a Coast too," Michael mutters.

So George loses his California connection and has to listen to Michael. Why didn't George send him up for the new production of *The Iceman Cometh*?! George answers: Because the soap opera star who got the part is "a name" and Michael Dorsey is only a name "when you want to send back a steak." Michael reminds George that he's done great work on the stage. Sure, says George, at the Harlem Theatre for the Blind, Strindberg in the Park, the People's Workshop in Syracuse; nothing with nothing. Michael reminds George that he got great reviews in Syracuse, "not that that's why I did it." Oh no, says George. God forbid Michael should lose his "standing as a cult failure."

The word has been spoken. "Failure."

George feels bad.

Michael says, "I sent you my roommate's play. It has a great part in it for me. Did you read it?"

"I'm your agent, not your mother!" says George. "I'm not supposed to find plays for you to star in. I'm supposed to field offers."

"Who told you that?" says Michael. "The agent-fairy?"

"Michael," George says, "nobody's going to do that play."

"Why?"

"Because it's a downer, that's why. Because nobody wants to produce a play about a couple that move back to Love Canal."

"But that actually happened!" Michael protests.

"Who gives a shit?!" yells George. "Nobody wants to pay twenty dollars to watch people living next to chemical waste. They can see that in New Jersey!"

Okay, Michael determines, he's willing to do anything now to raise money for the play: dog commercials, radio voice-overs, whatever George can get him.

But George says he can't get him anything, on any Coast, because he's just too difficult. He walked off the set when he was playing the dying Count Tolstoi because he wouldn't take direction from the mincing British director.

"Oh please," says Michael, "that was two years ago, and that guy is an idiot."

"They can't all be idiots, Michael," George answers. "You argue with everybody. You've got one of the worst reputations in this town . . . Nobody will hire you . . . I can't even send you for a commercial. You played a tomato for twenty seconds; they went half a day over schedule because you wouldn't sit down."

"Yes," Michael says. "It wasn't logical!"

"A tomato doesn't have logic!" George cries. "A tomato can't move!"

"That's what I said!" says Michael. "So if he can't move, how's he going to sit down?!"

George is losing his mind from this, so he suggests that Michael ought to get some therapy.

Michael says he's going to go out and get work and raise enough money to do the play without George's help.

"You're not going to raise twenty-five cents!" George fumes. "No one will hire you!"

"Oh yeah?" Michael says.

When next we see him, he's hard to see because he's crossing a New York street on the way to a soap opera audition and he looks like all the other women.

The give-and-take between Michael Dorsey and his agent George wouldn't have been anywhere near as much fun as it turned out to be if George had been a monster, and it would have been easy to make George a monster.

Agents own ten and sometimes fifteen per cent of everyone who's creative in America. If you don't have one, you don't work. On the other hand, you can't get one until you're working. Your agent tells you what you're doing wrong and why it's impossible to sell what you've done. Then when you go out and sell it on your own, your agent receives the checks and takes the percentage off the top before forwarding what's left to you. Many agents ultimately become very friendly with their clients. But the subtext of these relationships is often fraught with resentment. After all, selling is tacky; art is grand; but unsold art makes no one rich or famous or free enough financially to continue pursuing art as a career. So Michael Dorsey says to George Fields (in one version of *Tootsie*), "You're not my friend; you're my agent."

This line was cut from the movie, because it was so unfriendly as to be unfunny. Sydney certainly would have to understand, even share, the resentments of working artists who seethe and rankle at the power agents have over them. But seething and rankling belonged in another movie, and Sydney was always on guard lest bad blood between Michael and his agent spoil the comedy.

"The scene finally worked, I think, but in my honest opinion, it started off badly," Sydney explained. "Because he walked in with rage and you can't play comedy with rage. It was the rage of a rejected actor, *real* rage, and I don't think you will root for Michael with that."

"Sydney likes to think of Michael as self-destructive," said Dustin. "I like to think of him as heroic. When he tells people to fuck themselves, I think that's heroic. Because they're not interested in the work. They're interested in *success*. So, of course, he gets fired a lot . . . I'm doing this autobiographically. I got fired all the time when I was doing off-Broadway."

He was fired from a play called *Journey of the Fifth House* and was then rehired. He got an Obie. He was fired from *Sergeant Musgrave's Dance*. He says the first director of *Eh*, which brought Hoffman critical raves and the attention of Mike Nichols, wanted to fire him too.

"I was fired *usually* because I did not come up with the characterization fast enough. In other words, a shitty actor, the shittier actors, they give you a reading that is so slick and glossy, it's what they're gonna open with opening night. What you see is what you get. And a lot of directors and producers hire them. Because this is an art form *based on fear*. There's no *time*. If you're a perfectionist, then you're 'self-destructive' or 'difficult' or whatever; it's a dirty word: *perfectionist*, like you're sick. But what it means is you don't want it to be finished until it's finished. Until you know you have completed your best work on it. I asked this sculptor: When do you know you're done? He says: When I walk away from it. You've got to be able to say it's the best, the best I could do at that time.

"I gave very bad auditions. And then when I was hired, I tended to work underwater. Everybody else was acting up a storm and I was just mumbling around letting it grow. *If you do your work, it emerges.* If you do your work, the child you're raising grows up. You give it love, you say 'Be careful of fire' and things like that, but you don't say: This is your personality. You don't say to your wife: This is gonna be our marriage. And you don't treat creating a character any differently. It emerges. The trick is to leave it alone, to not *know* what's gonna happen. Like writers do that all the time; they say I can't wait to finish this book and find out how it turns out. That's what I do. Like this character Dorothy Michaels. She wasn't planned to come out this way, I didn't know how she was gonna turn out. You do that in the off-Broadway theatre in rehearsal and if you're an unknown, you scare the shit out of people.

"Ninety percent of the directors who work in the field don't know anything about actors. They don't take acting classes. They don't know. They say: (he says ferociously) Okay we'll *block* the first act now and in two days we're gonna *block* the second act. And what is blocking? It's the physical movement of the characters. How the fuck can you do the physical movement of the characters before the actors have *discovered* the characters?! Good directors tell the actors to sit around and talk and improvise . . .

"My anger is for myself and for other actors—that real good creative shit is cut off so much."

At the very beginning of *Tootsie*, before and behind the titles, Michael Dorsey's life as an actor is laid out in a montage of vignettes. He tries out for this role; that role. Out in the black theatre, invisible except for the cigar smoke collecting above their heads, the powers that are in charge of deciding whose "good creative shit" will live or die, say they want someone older. Michael says: "I can be older." They say they want someone younger. He says: "I can be younger." They say they want someone shorter. So he takes the lifts out of his shoes to show them he can be shorter. "Someone different," they say. "I can be different," he answers. "Someone else," they say.

There is no answer to that.

When he finally lands a role—the dying Count Tolstoi—he gets asinine advice from a British director who calls him "Love" and wants him to move downstage before expiring. Michael says that it doesn't make sense for Count Tolstoi to be able to move downstage when he's about to die. The director says: Do it because I said so. Michael throws down his script and walks off the stage.

Michael teaches an acting class. The kids in it do concentration exercises that civilians might find hilarious—sticking their tongues out at each other in slow motion. But this is very serious to Michael. Sandy Lester giggles while trying to sing off key. Michael demands sternly that she get control of herself. Later on in *Tootsie*, he coaches her for the soap opera and tries to awaken in her some approximation of rage. It isn't easy. "I have a problem with anger," Sandy says helplessly. But by calling her a bad actress, Michael finally succeeds in eliciting some wrath from Sandy. "Don't show me the anger," he says. "Just have it."

These takes from the inside of Dustin's past and art were very dear to his heart, particularly the acting class. It was shot at the loft on 18th Street, the one that was originally a ballet studio. (Dustin actually used to teach acting in an unused ballet studio.) For the acting class, Dustin and Sydney agreed to bring into the loft some real students of Jack Waltzer, a real acting teacher. In a series of shots unprecedented for their duration, Dustin delivered an impassioned lecture on acting to these young people. When he saw it in dailies, he loved it. It was so absolutely *real*. Finally, he was getting to play an actor, to show everyone what actors go through to learn their craft.

"I wanted this movie to be an homage to actors," Dustin recalled. (He says *oh-majh*, the French way, with the French meaning.) "Sydney says it's too inside, that nobody will appreciate that. But I think an audience can connect with anything that's universal. How to be a good actor—when you're trying to break through the frustration of that—I don't know if it's any different than *Rocky!*"

Despite the fact that the Screen Actors Guild would fine *Tootsie* for using non-union kids in the acting class scene, and despite the fact that he believed no film should begin with a lecture, Sydney authorized and supported the sequence. It did, however, leave him with an aching sense of déjà vu. "You know who was Jack Waltzer's teacher?" he said in his trailer at lunchtime. "In 1958? Me."

Just like Dustin, Sydney remembered the struggle to be an actor. However, he had ceased being inspired by it long ago, which was precisely why he hadn't *stayed* an actor. Dustin was having a won-

70

derful time returning to New York's ragged theatrical lofts; re-creating the agonizing, haphazard auditions; nailing the fascistic big shots under their cigar smoke. He appreciated the life-and-death battle against these brute forces, He wanted to be its *symbol!* It was still not forgotten in the theatre that when Dustin had accepted the Academy Award for *Kramer,* he had spoken encouragement to actors still battling.

But Sydney couldn't wait to get home to Los Angeles where he could nestle into the cutting room and reduce the almost 45 minutes of "homage" to a minute or so of vignettes before and among the titles, where they would set up the character of a man who is driven to put on women's clothes and thereby becomes a better man. Dustin wanted the class to anchor the theme of the whole film. Sydney mostly wanted one thematic strand from it—a moment equally precious to Dustin—a moment when Michael tells his stu-dents: "Don't play a part that's not in you." It was hoped that this one moment would help prepare the audience subliminally for the exchange at the end of the film when Julie says "I miss Dorothy" and Michael answers "She's right here."

"When I think the movie is hilariously funny," Sydney said, "is when there's an ingenuousness to Michael. When Michael says: 'I can be taller, I can be shorter,' my heart goes out to him. But if he says it—'Fuck you, I can be taller! Fuck you, I can be shorter! Fuck you, you don't know anything, you Establishment prick!'—I don't root for him any more.

"I mean, even in a picture like *Electric Horseman,* we had to be sure there wasn't one drop of real blood. The cops did stunts nobody can get up from. But we kept cutting back so you could see them dust themselves off. Because if Redford steals a horse and five cops are killed chasing him, *it's not funny.*

"I was having difficulty getting it through to Dustin that there can't be real blood. An argument full of rage and resentment differs from an argument-with-anger-that's-*comedic* because it rings so true and contains innocence."

Sydney's insistence on innocence, on Michael not hurting George and George not really hurting Michael, was once again classic theory ringing contemporary. Joe Weber and Lew Fields, the kings of burlesque comedy, had written a newspaper article on it in 1912:

"If a man . . . pokes his two forefingers into the eyes of another man without hurting them, then human nature will make you scream with mirth; not at the sight of the poking of the fingers into the other man's eyes . . . but because the man who had the fingers stuck into his eyes *might have been hurt badly but wasn't*. The greatest laughter, the greatest comedy, is divided by a hair from the greatest tragedy. Always remember that!"

Fidgety crew members, money-watching production managers might complain that Dusty and Syd were splitting hairs, but if they were, it was the all-important "hair" between comedy and tragedy they were splitting.

Sydney's role in the Michael-George scenes was immeasurably complicated because he was playing George. "It's hard for me to argue with him when I'm not behind the camera," Sydney mused. "Because I'm in the scene. And I feel much more capable of being objective about him than I feel capable of being objective about myself—because that's what I'm trained in." David ordered a video monitor, so Sydney could keep an eye on the scene while in it. "I'm going crazy in there watching myself watch myself," Sydney said.

The company observed Sydney's discomfiture with unbridled glee. "I love it when he's acting," said one crew member with a mischievous glint. "He gets nervous just like the other actors. The first day we shot him, his hands were shaking."

For his part, David McGiffert had no doubts that Sydney would bring off the role of George. "I've seen somebody do an extemporaneous reading for a scene," he commented, "and then I've seen Sydney stand in for that person and off the top of his head give the extemporaneous reading back *exactly*."

In the plush office, setting up for the take, Sydney sat uncomfortably at George Fields' big desk.

"Do I really need make-up just to rehearse, O?"

Owen said yes; because they had to set light levels.

"I don't have to change my pants, do I?" Sydney asked.

Owen and David said no.

"Just sit there and get nominated," said Dustin.

They ran through the "Tomato Scene."

Sydney tried to play it so that the basic affection between Michael and George survived this big confrontation, so that they would be able to pick themselves up from it and still be in a funny movie when it was over.

But Dustin tried the "Tomato Scene" with shaking, dancing rage, exploding like fireworks in the plush office. "You do good work and you're called crazy!" he yelled.

Then he tried it another way. With schtick. "I was a beefsteak tomato," he cried, "the sweetest, juiciest . . . nobody does vegetables like me!" And he stalked out, right into a closet.

Then he tried it another way. With vulgarity. With such a sincere, heartfelt rain of curses that the emotional level of the scene skyrocketed and Sydney was drawn into it and actually said "schmuck" on camera and had to stop himself from saying it again on the next take. The crew was loving every minute of the "Tomato Scene."

Between takes, Dustin ran into the crowded halls and talked to the people. They recharged him, like jumper cables. He grabbed a tall woman, forced her to the floor as though he were about to rape her, shouting, "She's only married a month to a guy with a .38 special, do you know what this is gonna cost me?!" The crowd laughed uproariously. Later he held a little Latin American girl on his lap with fatherly gentleness, writing what she wanted on his picture. A tall, grey-haired receptionist handed him a blank book. "My daughter said, you'd better get Dustin Hoffman's autograph, Ma, or else you're gonna have to bring him home with you." Two Chinese women stared at him from a respectful distance. It was his eyes, they said, he had the most beautiful eyes. He spied a sexy black woman in a pink blouse. "We'd have terrific children," he said to her. "Imagine. My nose and your cheekbones." And once again he loped toward the office door of George Fields for another take, looking back at the giggling woman with a wild and desperate meaning.

"Cut me off faster on the tomato," he said to Sydney.

"But then you'll say I'm cutting your tomato line . . ."

"It's okay, it's okay. Just don't cut me off when we do the close-ups."

Dustin used more and more of the hall to lope down before each take; like a marathon runner, he swooped past the only audience a film actor ever has, random strangers, and he took them inside himself and stored them, and when he faced Sydney Pollack across that fascistic big shot desk, they were there for him to draw on.

Then they settled down to do the scene again.

Dustin Hoffman, playing Michael Dorsey at a time in his career when he can't "get arrested" and wants very badly to go out and hit somebody, bursts into George Fields' office. George looks up, appalled at this intrusion. He is so startled that he actually loses his connection to the Coast. "God," said Sydney Pollack, viewing this scene at dailies. "I look like a frightened turtle."

No wonder he looked that way.

Michael Dorsey's thin body shakes. His face is on fire. "You do good work and you're called crazy for it!" he hollers. The normally calm and pleasant George loses control. His voice rises an octave. "A tomato doesn't have logic!" he screams. "A tomato can't move!"

The company, gathered in the tiny screening room at Technicolor where dailies were shown, burst into applause. Dustin was so happy with this work, with himself and Sydney, he bounced, he jiggled, he flopped down next to his director and yelled: "I'm beginning to love this movie!"

If the armature of *Tootsie* as Sydney saw it had to lead to Michael becoming a better man, then he had to be a bad guy to begin with. But nobody likes a bad guy. "And Michael's the hero of the picture," Sydney said, "you must root for him. You can't think of him as a mean guy who's fucking over two women (Julie and Sandy) at the same time, and that's what we're in danger of. Now. You've got two great weapons. One, you've got Dustin Hoffman. And two, he's funny. Anybody who can make you laugh, it's hard to hate.

"But I try to pretend that doesn't exist. Because that's not fair. That's like . . . if you're interested in the science of war and somebody just gives you more fire power, to me, you've still got to say: 'I want to win this *logically*.'"

This meant that Sydney was always setting up situations in which Michael Dorsey could be not bad but funny-bad; in which he could behave like a self-involved male chauvinist and still retain our sympathies by allowing us to laugh at him.

Michael takes Sandy to a party at the home of a big Broadway producer, but leaves Sandy's side to go and make passes at Julie, who is also a guest. However, Sandy isn't hurt. You might be upset with Michael if she were hurt. Instead, she heads directly for the opulent buffet, totally forgetful of Michael because she is so intent on eating all the free food. She even goes so far as to plunk grapes in her purse.

Michael on the terrace tells Julie that he finds her very interesting and would like to go to bed with her. She throws a drink in his face. However, that might make the scene too heavy; so Michael wipes his dripping face on the coattails of an innocent bystander.

Lest we think he is the *only* obnoxious male in Julie's life at that moment, this scene is carefully preceded by sub-scenes in which the Broadway producer tries to get Julie to go out with him by telling her lies about the big projects he has in store for her, and her date, Ron, runs into a woman he has recently been intimate with but completely forgotten.

These adjustments and finaglings kept *Tootsie* funny and took the curse off the dark side of Michael Dorsey's character, while still allowing it to show. In the same way, his relationship with Sandy was checked and balanced at every turn. "How will the audience know immediately that Teri is not the romantic leading lady?" Sydney asked. "Because unlike the structure of most pictures, in this one, you have first time love affairs with both women. In other words, he's not already having a known love affair with Teri. So you have to be super careful about how he and Teri go to bed. It has to be comedic enough and neurotic enough and unromantic and as funny as possible, so *you know* the real romance is with Julie."

On the night that Michael and Sandy go to bed with each other, therefore, she has taken a shower—because she feels so unsexy around him that she's sure he won't take it amiss. He feels so unsexy around her that he forgets that she is likely to reappear at any moment and starts trying on her clothes, to see if they would look nice on Dorothy. And when she comes out and finds him in his underwear, he thinks it might hurt her feelings if he doesn't say: "Uh . . . I want you, Sandy."

Sandy, who is not too bright in any case, says: "You do?"

Some of Dorothy Michaels' scenes got special attention from Sydney and Dustin because of their potential impact on Michael Dorsey's character. Like a rambunctious and intractable spinster sister, she had it in her power to make or break his reputation with the audience. And one scene between Dorothy and Ron was key to Michael's evolution into "a better man."

Ron has come to take Julie to dinner. Michael is there in his

Dorothy persona, ready to babysit for Amy. When Julie gets her coat, Ron and Dorothy are alone together for a moment. Ron takes the opportunity to ask point blank why Dorothy doesn't like him.

Dorothy says: I don't like you because of the way you treat Julie. You sneak around on her. You lie to her.

Oh, that, says Ron, looking just a bit perturbed, well, Dorothy, it's like this. When a woman wants me to seduce her, well, I usually do. But then she expects me to be exclusive, which of course, I'm not. And she starts behaving like I promised her something, which of course I didn't, but I'm such an easy touch, I can't help it, I start behaving like I promised her something too. But I can't tell her the truth because then, naturally, her feelings would be hurt. So it gets harder and harder and more and more complicated and surely now Dorothy you can see that it is me, Ron, the best director of daytime drama in television, who is the true and ultimate victim of this unfortunate syndrome.

Dabney Coleman could touch you to the core with this sad story. But he can't touch Dorothy. She says it's bullshit. She says she understands Ron a lot better than he thinks she does.

This scene with Dabney caused a big argument between Dustin and Sydney, which happened because, as David McGiffert would say in another context, Sydney was being "tenacious from the movie's point of view" and Dustin was being "tenacious from the character's point of view."

Dustin was playing Dorothy in this scene and Dorothy was a soft-core feminist. Dustin felt compelled to stand up for her political consciousness the same way he felt compelled to stand up for the color of her hair and the particular lines she ad libbed on her soap opera. Dorothy was his ultimate authority, and Dustin's instinct was to do what she would do and lambaste Ron for being a self-serving rotten chauvinist.

But Sydney's instinct as director was to preserve the good will of the viewing audience toward Michael Dorsey. And if Michael were to use Dorothy as a cover while taking a political stance he himself did not ascribe to, then we might dismiss Michael as a two-faced liar. "I kept saying: 'You can't be self-righteous!'" Sydney said. "Because you are lying to Julie, you are lying by being in a dress. You can't be a hypocrite! You have to say 'I understand you a lot better than you think I do' because you have been a liar too. You have to be stunned at the insight into yourself that he gives you, so that you can learn to be a better man yourself!"

In the final version of *Tootsie*, the armature Sydney wanted and the performance Dustin wanted were both on screen.

Collaboration is not always synonymous with compromise.

The loft where Michael Dorsey lived looked like Boston Harbor after the Fourth, and no untrained eye could differentiate one piece of garbage from the next. Dirty ashtrays. Broken furniture. Used books. Unwashed dishes. Potato chips. ("Don't eat them! They're in the next scene!")

Peter Larkin and his set crew had seen to it that in this, as in *Tootsie*'s other interiors, corners, recessed doorways, objects like refrigerators and occasional cacti cropped up to frame the shots with vertical lines. Without these, Larkin said, the anamorphic proportions of Panavision "would make one actor look like he's all alone in the Gobi Desert and two actors look like they're all alone in the Gobi Desert."

The most important vertical in the loft was a poster portrait of Samuel Beckett, author of *Waiting For Godot* and *Endgame*. He hung on Michael Dorsey's scruffy wall, evil-eyed and truculently black-and-white. Beckett's works had become modern classics in the theatre of the early '60s, just when Dustin was starting as an actor. He was considered one of the greatest avant garde playwrights in the world. And when Michael Dorsey stood next to that poster, with the same evil eye and determined independence, it was surely to catch a little of Beckett's glow.

Into the loft came a couple of dozen strangely assorted extras playing out-of-work actors, many of them wearing mismatched, re-assembled, junk clothing, and all of them praying in reality as in comedy for some kind of break. They hoped; they milled; they napped. They waited on the third floor until Joe Reidy, their baby-sitter, told them they were wanted on the fifth floor for shooting. Rumania Ford, who stored her make-up in a gilded tissue box, touched them up from time to time. Ruth Morley looked them over carefully. "Ask any designer this," she laughed, "they'll tell you, if there's any person you want to send home, that's the one who will end up right in front of the camera. So I'm always on the set whenever there are extras . . . I'll say to Joe (Reidy): This one is wearing something too much like Dustin, keep him away; this one is terrific, try to get him in the middle. It's an absolute disease of ADs to put your least favorite in the front row. Thank God the ADs on this picture are so wonderful."

Add to the mess and the extras Bill Murray. This lumbering comedian had been very funny in *Caddyshack* in which he played a golf course janitor trying unsuccessfully to eliminate one gopher; in *Stripes* during which he unhinged several armies; and in *Meatballs* in which he played a lunatic head camp counselor.

Although in *Tootsie* Murray was portraying the other-worldly playwright named Jeff who shared the loft with Michael, off-screen he was still doing head counselor. "Owen!" he cried in the dark screening room at dailies. "Why can't you give me a shadow like Orson Welles'?!"

Michael and Jeff support themselves by working as waiters in the same chic restaurant. One night after work, they walk home down a dark wet street. Michael says he is not depressed. He has not mentioned the fact that it is his birthday, he explains to Jeff, because age has no effect on character actors. Obviously, he is very depressed. He opens the loft door. Flips on the light. SURPRISE! all the out-of-work actors yell. HAPPY BIRTHDAY! they sing.

Jeff, who planned the whole thing, grins like a buddha in the background.

The "Surprise Party Scene" was critical in setting up many of the thematic strands in Michael Dorsey's character. We had to see him picking up girls, dumping girls, being dumped by them; a loveless life; an aging bachelor in poverty. Yet, the scene was especially hard to do because whatever script there may have been was not being used and because Sydney and Dustin were mostly concocting it on their feet.

Sydney set up "a wild shot" of Michael sitting at the piano, playing occasional music of his own creation, in order to prepare for when Dustin, as Dorothy Michaels, plays the piano for Les and Julie up at their farm.

And Sydney ordered a baby. She came on her father's back in a knapsack. He wanted to concoct a shot in which Michael displays his indifference toward an adorable baby, so that later on when he displays tenderness to Julie's infant daughter Amy, we would see that he had grown into something of a better man.

Sydney asked for a rehearsal.

"The baby doesn't have to be in for rehearsal," announced the considerate David McGiffert.

"That baby is a pro!" Bill Murray hollered. "The baby has to learn! Bring the baby back!" They rehearsed the scene. They did a few takes. By the third "SURPRISE! HAPPY BIRTHDAY!," the extras had begun to lose their sparkle. "You realise, Sydney," said Bill with droll ferocity, "this baby is sucking everybody's energy right out of the room!"

"Folks," Sydney said, "please make it a little tougher for Dustin to get you quiet. If you stop yelling the minute he starts talking, it's a little cue-y."

"Okay everybody, touch the sky!" Bill Murray hollered.

Surprise! they yelled. Happy Birthday! they sang. Surprise! Happy Birthday! Surprise!

"Save it," said Sydney.

"Please, folks," said David.

Sydney walked into the cactus.

A pair of Dustin's custom-made $175 falsies disappeared.

Trying to keep track of the matching and the props in a room bursting with new people who might at any time relocate, or even swipe, something crucial, and who were always receiving new lines, Renee Bodner the script supervisor was having a hell of a day.

Dustin Hoffman was completely surrounded by "bits and pieces," the random junkyard realism of the movie set: tiny takes, nameless extras, forgettable lines right out of life. However, the actor wasn't on a movie set, not in his heart. He was back in the theatre. Samuel Beckett was on his wall. And on his dressing table, he had a playbill, dated January 31, 1965, for *A View from the Bridge* by Arthur Miller. The cover design was by Ben Shahn. The director was Ulu Grosbard. The cast included Jon Voight, Robert Duvall, Susan Anspach, Richard Castellano. The assistant director was Dustin Hoffman. This aging playbill wasn't in *Tootsie*, but Dustin kept it on the set as a constant reminder of the glorious bad old days before everybody got into the movies.

The very last scene in *Tootsie* takes place on Theatre Row, on West 42nd Street. In one version of a Gelbart script, Michael accosts Julie as she heads east from National Video, past Playwrights' Horizons and The Lion Theatre and the Harold Clurman. He wants to see her, he says. He wants it to be again the way it was when he was Dorothy and they talked and they trusted each other. "Listen, the hard part's over," he says. "We were already best friends. Don't hold it against me that I wear pants."

A group of tourists, with a child, approach Julie, asking for her autograph. The little boy looks up at Michael.

"Are you anybody?" he asks.

"Am I anybody?" Michael answers, "Me? Are you kidding? I've been a woman, an old man, a prince of Denmark! I've been Romeo and Cyrano! I've been Willy Loman! Am I anybody?! I'm *everybody*! I'm an actor, man!"

FREEZE, it says in the old script.

These lines were cut from the movie.

But as Sydney Pollack had said of other cut lines, they continued to "bleed colors" on *Tootsie* as a whole, and most particularly upon Michael Dorsey's struggle to be loved.

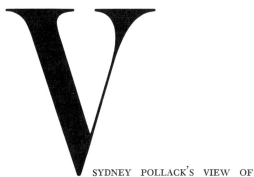

SYDNEY POLLACK'S VIEW OF
producing was defensive. He didn't admit to liking it. But he said that producing was the only way he knew to preserve his vision of the movie in an ultimate sense and to guard his directorial decisions against invasion and change. "I would much rather somebody else do the producing," he explained. *"But I do it because it buys me freedom.* I don't want to have to explain, ask permission . . ."

Like the driver of an armored truck, he watched constantly for any sign of danger, *expecting* it, ignoring no detail that might invite trouble. Would a certain slant in a certain newspaper or magazine article hurt *Tootsie*'s public image? Would a certain character in a certain situation offend the movie's audience? Would a certain scene endanger the PG rating *Tootsie* had to have to draw the family trade at the Christmastime release date? What were the political risks inherent in the movie's theme? How could they be avoided? *All of this* was producing, as Sydney defined it.

He was very concerned that the film should be placed correctly in terms of public relations. He didn't want to lose any advantage *Tootsie* might gain from keeping Dustin's disguise a surprise as long as possible, and insisted that Dorothy's look not be leaked until late in the shoot, and then only to media picked specifically for that purpose.

But Dustin insisted that an actor as proud of his work as Michael Dorsey would barge into the very center of theatrical action to test and prove his disguise, just as soon as he had fooled the soap opera people and won the role of Emily Kimberly. And because Michael wanted to test in public, Dustin wanted to test in public.

So one day three women had lunch at the Russian Tea Room. They were Lisa Hoffman, Renee Schisgal (Murray's wife and Dustin's business partner), and Dorothy Michaels. Ms. Michaels stopped by at the table of John Springer, a seasoned show business press agent, and introduced herself as "an aspiring poet-ingenue from Kansas City." (The words of *Time* Magazine.) Springer was completely fooled. "I knew there was something fascinating about the woman," he said. "I just didn't know what." Dorothy also fooled Jon Voight, who had been in *Midnight Cowboy* with Dustin and had known him since the old production of *A View from the Bridge*.

Sydney was understandably nervous about these shenanigans. But they worked; so what was there to say?

Everybody got a laugh out of the Voight and Springer episodes. However, the adventures of Dorothy Michaels in Fort Lee, New Jersey in May 1982 proved less amusing. For the scene in which Dorothy and her soap co-stars sign autographs in a suburban shopping center, Ezra Swerdlow, the location manager, had selected the Plaza West Shopping Center. About 120 people, including 50 extras to portray shoppers, were bussed in from New York, which is only a hop away from Fort Lee over the George Washington Bridge.

They arrived at about 6 a.m. Sydney had hoped to keep the news photographers away from Dustin as he dressed and made up as Dorothy, to preserve the surprise of Dustin's look until much later in the publicity campaign for the movie.

The *Tootsie* people kept quiet, but personnel of the shopping center, which had been paid $500 for the use of part of its parking lot by the film, leaked the news for all it was worth. "I don't mind people knowing Dustin plays a woman," Sydney told the *Star-Ledger* of Newark. "That's bound to get out. But I don't want anyone to know *what* he looks like . . . I want you to pay $5.00 and see him as a woman. I don't want his picture to be in 150 million papers." Crew members covered Dustin with an umbrella, but the photographers circumvented it and Dorothy's face was soon out all over the Metropolitan area. By the end of the day, Sydney had accepted the inevitable and was trying to make friends with the press again. "You have your job to do," said the director of *Absence of Malice.* "We have ours."

There were other publicity snags. Sydney and Dustin were hoping for a well-timed *Life* magazine cover featuring Dustin as Dorothy and Dustin as Dustin. But *Life* tested the cover and found that it did not sell as well as others, particularly the photo of a doctor holding a human liver that eventually beat Dorothy off the cover. As for interviews, they made both Dustin and Sydney nervous. Janet Maslin of the *New York Times* visited the set and collected material for a story, and until it actually appeared and proved to be charming, they didn't stop worrying about it. Like many celebrities in an era of wildly imaginative journalism, Sydney and Dustin were spooked by reporters. You never knew what they were going to say about you.

For *Tootsie,* a Columbia picture, this situation was immeasurably complicated by the appearance during the shoot of David McClintock's fastidiously researched book, *Indecent Exposure.* In the book stores in July, excerpted in *Esquire,* it was accepted as truthful, and yet its emergence made all associated with *Tootsie* even more jittery around the press. When the shy young Parisian reporter from *Le Figaro* (who had probably never heard of the *National Enquirer*) approached Dustin, he was friendly but somewhat discouraging. "Hi. How are you?" he said. "How's the anti-Semitism in France? Still good?"

Sydney pretty much believed that it was impossible to write the truth and not hurt anyone, as the newspaper editor in *Absence of Malice* had said, and journalistic publicity therefore was something he tried to control as much as generate.

Sydney tried as well to control the rating that *Tootsie* would get. The film was due to open just before Christmas, when the nation's kids were home from school and the nation's families were eager to take in a flick on a cold snowy day. No nudity or violence or explicit sex was ever called for by this comedy. But the language, being true to life, included a couple of "Fuck you's" in what was one of the most light-hearted comic scenes in the film.

Sandy has brought Michael along to her soap opera audition "to enrage her."

"Fuck you," he says.

"Thank you," she says.

"Fuck you," he says.

"God bless you," she says, and off she goes to her reading.

In November, the ratings board met about *Tootsie* and gave it an R. Sydney appealed. The decision was reversed. *Tootsie* got her PG only a few weeks before opening.

The most difficult aspect of producing concerned money. Right before *Tootsie* went into production, Coca-Cola had completed its acquisition of Columbia Pictures, one in a number of forays into film producing by large non-film corporations. "There are probably more people on Wall Street who consider themselves experts on Hollywood than on Detroit," wrote Stephen Sansweet in *American Film*. "Why? 'It's more fun than just about anything else going on today,'" one Wall Street analyst answered.

Coca-Cola had taken over Columbia in the post-Begelman shake-ups, at a time when the industry as a whole was showing a marked decline in profitability for studios. In 1979, film and television divisions among the "seven majors" had pre-tax profits of $640 million. In 1980, it was $477 million. In 1981, it was $301 million. About half as many film starts occurred in 1982 as in 1981. Still, the possibilities for profit were enormous, even with the huge salaries of stars and other "above the line" personnel. "I suppose nobody is worth the amount of money they're getting, in philosophical terms," Sydney told *Variety*. "But if you're responsible for making the kind of money some of these films make, then actually you are worth it. . . . If Clint Eastwood, for instance, makes ten films, all of which bring in over $25 million domestically, you can't argue with what he's getting paid."

In his trailer on 18th Street, outside the loft set, Sydney ate his Pritikin lunch and tried to explain "movie money." "Movie money," he said, "doesn't work the way we normally think money works, that ten million makes twenty million. No, ten million makes a hundred million if you do it right. You have $10 million coming in for this picture and somebody'll float you a loan for $50 million and you do three pictures at $15 million apiece with the $50 million and two of them flop and the third one hits and does $60 million.

So then you've paid back the original ten *and* all the money that was in the flops, and you invest the remainder in CD's at twenty percent or you pick up a little company that makes vinyl for records . . .

"Now Columbia was doing all right before Coca-Cola," he said between gulps of his sea green lime drink. "Because the studio really had a great year last year. In the Begelman years, they started to pay down this horrible debt that they had. Under Frank Price (Columbia's chairman), they kept on doing well."

He finished his zucchini and was now into a large wooden bowl of lettuce and tomatoes, dressed only with some low-sodium vinegar.

"Frank Price is one of the few studio heads in the business who's ever held a creative post. Frank was a writer. I've known him for twenty years. He's a businessman, he ran the television department at Universal. But still, he began as a writer. He knows what it means to make act one and act two and act three. (When Sydney left the theatre, there were still three acts in most plays.) So you can have a reasonable creative conversation with him."

Reasonable though executives might be, the actual numbers involved in movie-making seemed irrational to laymen. How could so much money be spent at such phenomenal losses? It was a question the recession public might well ask of its government, its defense industry, its Chrysler Corporation, its movie industry. Plain people would be hard pressed to understand how any set of individuals could spend $10 million dollars and make $25 million dollars and *still* not turn a profit.

"Profits are an invention of bookkeeping," Sydney said, leafing through his lettuce. "Pictures make a lot of money and never go into profits.

"So. If a picture costs $10 million and does twenty-five, how come it doesn't make a profit of fifteen?

"The fact is, it doesn't.

"Because, the fact is, if a picture costs $10 million, the interest to borrow the ten million for a year is two million. If it's two years from the time you borrow the ten until money starts coming back, then it's four million. That's fourteen. For a $10 million picture, most companies seriously will spend eight to ten million for prints and advertising. If you spent four on interest, ten on prints and advertising, you're at twenty-four so far. Right? Now wait.

"Columbia Pictures has branch offices all over the world. Who pays them? Columbia's not a philanthropist. So they have a system. They charge a distribution fee. They say okay, you make a picture, our fees are thirty, thirty-five, and forty.

"Thirty percent in the United States; thirty-five percent in Canada; forty percent foreign; this is what it costs them and, therefore, you to have your picture distributed.

"If $5.00 comes in at the box office and it's in the opening week, you have a 90–10 deal, then $4.50 goes to Columbia and $.50 goes to the exhibitor. If it's in the fifth week, it's down to 70–30, then you get $3.50 on each $5.00. But of the $3.50 that comes in, Columbia takes a thirty percent fee off the top, to pay for buildings in Paris, typewriters, phone bills, employees all over the world marketing the picture.

"Now you have to say, if your picture costs ten and the hard dollars you've spent are twenty-four, what amount of money do you have to make to be able to take thirty percent off the top and still have twenty-four left to pay back the hard dollars?

"If you earn, say, thirty-five million, you take ten off and give it to the distribution company; you take four and pay it to the bank; take ten or eleven and give it to the newspapers and the networks for the ads, it's $2000 a print for a thousand prints—that's another two million.

"*You've spent $10 million on the picture but you don't break even until you've gotten back $35 million.*"

As for "a piece of the picture," that's another concept which, like "profits," has only a vague and foggy place in the public consciousness. "A piece of the picture" means "a percentage of the gross" which both Dustin and Sydney have on *Tootsie.*

"When you first start out in the business, you get only up-front money. You don't get percentages.

"Next thing you're entitled to is what they call net profits which are practically non-existent in most pictures. So if you have four and a half percent of the net profits, it's very hard to make any money. But as you grow more successful, you can ask for a piece of the gross.

"Now gross is not box office. Nobody collects off box office. Everybody thinks you do. The $5.00 that goes into the box office doesn't have anything to do with me or Dustin (or Charles Evans or Dick Richards or Don McGuire, etc., etc.). We're collecting off of what Columbia gets. Not what the box office gets. We don't own the box office. That's owned by Mr. Plitt or Mr. Sutton Theatres . . . those guys get rich too on hits. What comes into the studio is called *film rentals,* and that's what your deal is predicated on.

"So the next time you hear that so and so got ten percent of the gross, it means he got ten percent of the money that came into the studio from film rentals. Not ten percent of the money that came into the box office."

What Sydney simplified with his characteristic energy and logic was really the stuff of unbearable pressure. Profits. Grosses. Percentages. Iron-clad release dates. Daily, detailed reports to the studio accounting for every penny. These bottom lines had haunted *Tootsie* like future-shock all summer. He would have to have the film in some kind of shape to show exhibitors from the non-blind bidding states by mid-October. He would have to have a work print for crucial members of the critical media to preview in mid-November. He would have to have *Tootsie* out everywhere by Christmas. The editing staff in Burbank was already working around the clock, piecing together the dailies that were flown in from New York every day, preparing a rough assembly so that Sydney could get to work on the final editing as soon as the last shot was fired. Originally, *Tootsie* had been projected at a cost of $19,764,946. It would come in finally at $21,019,940, "excluding a 12½% studio overhead charge," *Variety* said, "and interest which would put the figure in the mid-twenties." That meant that although the film would be about $1,250,000 over budget, the overage would fall within 10% (a Hollywood acceptable).

"Listen," Ron Schwary said. "If the picture makes money, nobody remembers what you went through, okay? On *Electric Horseman,* we had weather problems, I can't *tell* you what weather problems we had. But *Electric Horseman* did very well at the box office and nobody remembers the problems now except me and Sydney. If this picture bombs, I can tell you right now, names will fly, I'll be up shit creek, Sydney, Dustin, the make-up, the wardrobe people. . . . If this picture does good, Dustin will be praised, Sydney will be praised, we'll all be heroes."

Most people would have loathed the lunch Sydney had just finished. But he ate it with gusto—because he was sure it was the food he needed for survival. "Look, two and two is four," he said. "Once you learn that, you know your way around numbers. The part of the business you can control is the business part. You have to be a fanatic about that. So you can be totally free to wander and be haphazard in the other area where the creativity is."

He grinned. He pushed the empty bowl out of his way. "*Anything* is easier than art," he said.

In no aspect of producing was Sydney more defensive than the political aspect. "I don't, I desperately don't want a bunch of feminists after me for depicting two helpless ladies being victimized by macho men," he said. "So I'm in a little hot water here . . ."

Both he and Dustin explained that the movie had originated in the ferment of feminist awakening. They knew, therefore, that it was going to have to navigate political minefields, that any political statement in text or subtext would have to be produced with a light hand, a good heart and the utmost sensitivity to the feelings of women in the audience. "I so don't want this movie to be . . . what's the word . . . meretricious," Sydney said. "It happens often in films and I hate it. Hollywood's full of directors who think they're philosophers, great thinkers, they're doing things of 'import.' It's what I got scared to death of in *The Way We Were*. And I've got the same problem here.

"Michael puts on a dress and it's 1982. Everybody in the audience is on guard, watching, asking: what are you saying about masculinity? What are you saying about femininity?

"You say: 'Pass me the cream.' Perfectly innocent.

"But if the atmosphere is sexually political, then that's an inflammatory remark. So the woman answers: 'Get it yourself!' "

Both the producer and the star tried to look deeply into the "sexually political atmosphere" around *Tootsie*. They read feminist books. They consulted feminist friends. They thought hard about their wives and daughters. Dustin concentrated on understanding women by *being Dorothy*. Sydney concentrated on understanding women by sniffing the air outside the *Tootsie* set and coming in with a temperature reading.

"Granted, *Tootsie* isn't a definitive treatise on what a woman is,"

Sydney said. "Michael doesn't know shit about being a woman. But at least he can say in the end: 'I learned something about myself; I've just got to be able to do it without the dress.'"

They concentrated. They tried. But it wasn't so easy to "do it without the dress," not when you had been brought up to be a chip off the old patriarchy.

Dustin habitually talked about sex with women in the most graphic terms, and some of the time he was being funny, but some of the time he wasn't. And the toughest, most resilient of women felt discomfited by this, suspecting they were being tested somehow or deliberately embarrassed, the better to be managed and controlled.

Sydney invariably referred to women as "honey" and "dear." There were some women on the set who could not remember ever having been referred to by name by Sydney. And although it was silly to make a big Federal case out of something so dumb and stupid and unimportant, still, as Teri Garr once commented, it was noticed every time it happened.

One of the biggest potential sexual trouble spots in *Tootsie* was the character of Sandy Lester, Michael's student and lover. Teri Garr is an innately funny actress, and as Sydney himself had pointed out, funny is easy to love. He worried that "you're gonna like Teri Garr too much," that she was "sweet," that "you're gonna feel sorry for her" when Michael treats her badly. So when Sydney worked on the character of Sandy he adjusted her lines, and her reactions, even the way she looked, so that she would not command our sympathies too much and become a symbol of female oppression.

Teri meanwhile was having to make some adjustments of her own, in her life outside the movie, adjustments that were augmenting the captivating insecurity of Sandy Lester. She was chafing at always being cast as the second lead. Her big breakthrough into top billing came with Francis Ford Coppola's *One from the Heart* but that didn't break her through. When she first heard of *Tootsie*, she asked her agent to send her up for it. He checked and returned with the answer that there was nothing in it for her. A few months later, when Sydney called, Teri got mad at her agent because there *was* something in it for her after all. In time, Teri understood that until Elaine May rewrote the role of Sandy, it probably had not been suitable. But Teri wanted the lead. On her way to a courtship lunch with Sydney, she vowed she was not going to accept second banana woman again. "I'm going to play their game," she said to herself. "I'm going to say 'no.' And then I said to myself, come on, you're an actress! An actress *acts*! This is Dustin Hoffman! This is Sydney Pollack! What am I doing thinking of turning down this role?! And then he was so honest with me, Sydney. He knew exactly how I felt, where I was at. He was so honest with me that I couldn't refuse him."

The men on the *Tootsie* crew were crazy about Teri. Whenever her shots came up, they would call out—in happy mockery of "big star" treatment—"Miss Garr! Oh, Miss Garr! You are want-ed!" Perhaps her popularity was due in part to her vulnerability and self-doubt, which mirrored the feelings of crew members who were themselves unsure of their future. Checking in at their unions, seeing their friends and skilled colleagues on unemployment lines, many of them had no idea whether there would be another movie in their futures. David McGiffert, for example, was a man whose first major motion picture had been *King Kong*, whose last one had been *An Officer and a Gentleman*, and who had not stopped working in between and could expect with reason to go on forever as long as there was a film industry. Yet he testified, "As we're sitting here, I don't know whether I'll ever work again.

"It's very weird," McGiffert continued. "I have a wonderful cycle. I'm off for maybe a month or two months. When I start back to work, I go: God, I've forgotten everything I know, I'll never be able to do it again. Then I start working and I realize I can do it and I think God, I'm never gonna be able to last. And then I finish and I think oh God, I'm never gonna work again.

"That's the cycle.

"For a lot of film people."

In rooting for Teri, the self-doubters in the company rooted for themselves. She radiated insecurity and satirized it at the same time, taking the curse off it, making it a role . . . not just Sandy Lester's role but her own, in her own life. And as long as it was just a role, the possibility existed that it might not always have to be played.

Just as agents were courting the rising star of Dorothy Michaels, they were courting Teri. The famous Sam Cohn of International Creative Management took her to lunch at the Russian Tea Room. He tempted her. She was so nervous about this temptation that she stopped in at a yogurt bar and continued to eat even though she had just eaten at the Russian Tea Room. "It's more money," she said, munching on a carob chip. "The more powerful your agent is, the more money you are going to get."

Teri had grown up the daughter of a widow in Los Angeles. Her mother worked "in the studios," in wardrobe, and Teri recalled that she earned much less in those days than men earned for the same job. Teri could remember receiving as a child the beautiful clothes cast off by successful actresses.

"I want to be on top," she said. "Everybody wants to be on top. But I don't think I'll ever be on top because nobody takes me seriously. I used to be a dancer. I did the road tour of *West Side Story* with the original cast. I worked my ass off dancing. *I broke my nose!* Then they gave me one line. And I said it. And it got a laugh! I couldn't believe how easy it was to get that laugh. So I studied acting."

She moseyed along 57th Street, fit and tan and pretty. People on the street did double takes at her, knowing they had seen her somewhere, but where? "I've come so far," she mused. "I started with my ass hanging out, a chorus dancer, and now when I go on *The Tonight Show,* I try to sneak in these little remarks to support the women's movement. And they smile and they laugh, and I don't think they hear me."

Teri may have been on the brink of stardom, but she was keenly aware of being on the verge of oblivion. "If you stop pushing, for one minute, they forget you. You're out. Gone. Goodbye. I don't know what to do about Sam Cohn. I want to be a big star, I do. But . . ."

She didn't want to hurt her agent's feelings and abandon a tested relationship.

She didn't want to be "on the bottom of the heap" in a whole stable full of Cohn's more famous clients, people like Meryl Streep, Roy Scheider, Bob Fosse.

She wondered if she would ever be taken seriously.

She thought maybe she ought to marry and have children soon. "Only twelve more shopping days 'til Christmas," she quipped ironically.

Teri was pleased with her work in *Tootsie.* However, one evening she laughed that Sydney was going to bar her from dailies. "He says all I do is look at my face!" she said. "I mean I am so vain! I look and I say, well, harumph, I'm never gonna hold my head *that* way again. I don't know when this happened to me. I didn't use to be this way." And then she went on to say what a jerk she was, how silly she was being; of course, Sydney was only kidding around with her.

But Owen Roizman said Teri "didn't know how right she was" to be concerned about her looks in the movie.

"The first day I worked with Teri, I made her look beautiful," he recalled. "I mean really great. She even stood up and complimented me, gave me a really big 'Thank you!' I felt very good about it.

"But Dustin and Sydney said, 'You made her look too good. She doesn't look like the character. She's too pretty. It's not right.'

"So what I tried to do after that was compromise a little bit and just try to make her look decent. See, I can make anybody look much better than they normally look. Or much uglier. It's in the lighting."

He said this with far more guilt than pride. Maybe he was hoping that after *Tootsie* was over, somebody would tell Sandy the truth.

After Michael and Sandy have begun a sexual relationship she is ignored and avoided by him, not because he wants to hurt her but because he is too busy doing Dorothy and falling in love with Julie to have any time left in his life for Sandy. He has told her that they cannot see each other because he has a terrible cold. She believes him. The cold lasts *for days* (while he pursues his other life as a soap opera star.) But she believes him. It's such a bad, catching cold that they have to rehearse Jeff's play *over the phone*. Still, Sandy believes him.

Finally Sandy shows up at the loft, irate, up to here with Michael's behavior. You have not answered my phone calls, she says. The answering machine was broken, he says. She gives him her "I've heard this shit before" look and asks him outright if he's gay.

"In what sense?" he answers.

She wants THE TRUTH, dammit! Enough of these stories. They are demeaning! She'd *prefer* the truth! Once before, in *Tootsie*, a woman told Michael Dorsey that she would prefer the truth. It was Julie and she was saying to Dorothy that really, it would be refreshing if the next guy who came on to her would just come out and say: "You're interesting and I'd like to make love to you." The next time he sees her in his Michael persona, he says: "You're interesting and I'd like to make love to you." She throws a drink in his face.

However, it would be silly for Michael to expect the same kind of behavior from Sandy. After all Julie is a grown-up. Sandy is an emotional child. He sits down next to her at the table and takes a lot of beats and blurts out: I'm in love with another woman.

Teri Garr, knowing Sandy Lester, wanted to react to this with hurt and self-hatred.

Dustin Hoffman, knowing what Dorothy Michaels would do, wanted Sandy to react with outrage and anger.

Sydney Pollack, not wanting this film to be about "helpless ladies victimized by macho men," wanted Sandy to react the way he thought a "mature" woman would react, the way *Julie* reacted, namely, with outrage and anger.

Teri tried to get the anger, because it was wanted, but she couldn't, because she didn't really believe in it. Sydney explained and encouraged. "Let's try it again, honey," he said. Dustin fed her not lines but subtext, trying to enrage her in more or less exactly the same way as Michael had enraged Sandy during their coaching session the night before the soap opera tryout.

"You're not gonna be a little baby now," he goaded. "You're not gonna go crazy when you hear the truth like a little baby."

A small cloud of annoyance began to appear on Teri's face, but though she tried, she couldn't get angry.

Sydney said that if it was angry, it would be funny, and once again he explained why.

Teri roamed the loft. This was a big scene for her, and it wasn't working, and she was irritated. She found a grey hair on her blonde head and displayed it to Joe Coscia the hair stylist with grim irony. Dustin made an announcement that Teri needed a few moments to prepare, so the camera should please be patient.

They did another take.

"Okay, you're gonna get the truth," Dustin said. *"I'm in love with a better actress!"*

"Don't say other lines, Dustin!" Teri snapped furiously. "Please! You confuse me!"

"Okay. Here it is. The truth. I'm in love with another woman."

Teri screamed.

93

She leaped from the table; she practically knocked it over.

Michael gets terrified. "Sandy, I'm crazy about you. You're one of the dearest friends I've ever had. But let's not pretend it was something else. We're gonna lose everything we had."

"I never said 'I love you'!" Sandy screams. "I don't care about 'I love you'. I read *The Second Sex*! I read *The Cinderella Complex*! I'm responsible for my own orgasms. I don't care. I just don't like to be *lied* to!"

"Save it," Sydney called.

The crew burst into cheers and applause.

"Was that dynamite?!" Dustin yelled. "Now how many guys would want to jump into bed with *that*?! You'd think twice, wouldn't you, heh heh . . . the underside of Garr."

Teri laughed. She shook her head helplessly. For a moment, the famous expression returned to her face; but then it disappeared, and she went on with her work. "Most of the time," she said sardonically at dailies, "I succumb in the end and just do 'girl.'"

In fact, it was no joke that when a woman deviated from the appearance of insecurity, many a man would think twice about going to bed with her. "Doing girl," as Teri put it, was a kind of foreign policy by which a huge chunk of *Tootsie*'s female audience habitually put men at ease.

However, the real woman behind the traditional cover was now so exposed by literature and the media and plain communication among individuals that she had become an open secret. Whether she was the "real" Teri Garr or the "real" Jessica Lange or movie extra homemakers watching Dorothy Michaels on television and saying "Now, there's a real woman," she was the final conscience of the movie. She was the reason that Sydney Pollack had to constantly judge the political impact of Sandy Lester. She was the reason he felt compelled to keep Teri Garr's spur-of-the-moment, ad libbed Cinderella complex tirade in the final version of the movie.

Like so many women in the late-feminist social milieu, Teri Garr felt ambivalent. The ideal of a woman who was an independent, striving, self-realized person was so much a part of her life and times that it could never be denied again. But it was so hard to stand up for that woman, it was murder. The old patriarchy, much esteemed in the performing arts where monolithic leadership by *one* creative man was thought to be essential, crawled like a primaeval mist over the boards of show business, obscuring the path toward independence. It was *so hard* not to be nostalgic for that mist. One day at her famous script interpretation class, Stella Adler—the ideological enemy of Lee Strasberg and one of the few Group Theatre founders still active—was talking about Strindberg. She was discussing *The Father* and the old patriarchy. Stella was well over 80; the feminist ideals that made Teri Garr feel nervous, even guilty every time she didn't argue as much as Dustin Hoffman, were not part of her life and times. In trying to capture the essence of the patriarchy for her class of young, out-of-work actors, Stella suddenly stopped talking about Strindberg and started telling a story about Max Reinhardt, the great impressario.

It was opening night, she said. The actors were in their dressing rooms, tense, jittery. The audience was gathering in the great Berlin theatre. The actors felt nervous. They suddenly couldn't remember anything they had learned to do at rehearsal. Their hands were shaking. Through the backstage area came Max Reinhardt. He looked in on each member of the cast. He smiled, fatherly and sympathetic. And he gave each actor a piece of candy. Just recalling this incident brought tears to Stella's eyes. But she was the only one in her class who cried. Times had changed. If Sydney Pollack had given his actors pieces of candy, he would probably have encountered as much rage as gratitude. Patriarchal attitudes were no longer acceptable or even likeable. But what style should replace it? What was "the new likeability"? It was hard for either men or women to say . . . because their view of the situation was so obscured by the mist of nostalgia, which had not yet been cleared by the winds of change.

"I love Sandy's exit line," Sydney said. " 'I don't take this shit from friends. Only lovers!' It's true, it's so true. You only get hurt by people you love! Not by your good friends, otherwise they wouldn't be your friends. You'd get rid of them in two seconds!

"One of the biggest differences that I can think of between my generation and the generation now was that we thought mystery was a corollary of romance. Sex was a mystery. We coveted not knowing. There was something sort of minimally hostile associated with any sexual attraction. You had a best girlfriend if you were a girl. You had a best friend if you were a guy. *Then* you had your lover."

Sydney's personal break with that tradition had occurred through the catalyst of his own marriage. In the late '60s, he and his wife

Claire had separated for about a year. She was an actress who had given up a promising career to raise her family. "She was the typical example of the woman who took it and took it and then exploded," Sydney said. "Like a volcano. The first thing that happened was that she threw me out of the house. I kept saying: 'Wait a minute! This is my house!' But I went. I kept thinking: What has happened to this quiet, meek, beautiful wife I had? She's turned into a maniac. . . .

"See, I grew up with a father who was the center of the pyramid. So I had these old-fashioned ideas about what a man was and what a woman was."

He went off to Europe to work with John le Carré on a movie that was never made. "And when I came back, we sort of started to date," he said. "And we found there was a way of repositioning. She really fought for that space she wanted."

Claire Pollack, without even a high school diploma, went back to school for eight years and became an architect. The home she created on Lola and Robert Redford's Utah spread has become a showcase for students of solar design.

"I don't know the real answer to what is masculine and what is feminine," Sydney concluded. "All we have to go on, really, is what we've been taught culturally. But it somehow seems wrong not to understand these things better. Making *Tootsie* is about wanting to know, wanting to be more useful as a person, wanting not to go on being dumb about life . . . and people. . . ."

THE "WRAP PARTY" FOR THE *Tootsie* production company took place on Friday, August 27 at a glittering disco by New York's Hudson River. There was food and drink and dancing, and the sense of release was as palpable as the cool breeze of oncoming fall. Men who had never been seen in anything but working clothes wore spiffy jackets and gold chains; wives and husbands who had never been met before were introduced all around. Dustin Hoffman, lover of the proletariat, friend to grips and gaffers, came with his wife, Lisa, and relaxed with the company. But Sydney Pollack wasn't at the party. He had closed up the shoot at one o'clock that afternoon, caught the 4:30 plane and was now flying the night away to California, where *Tootsie* would be edited into its final shape.

A rough assembly of *Tootsie* had already been put together by her editors, Fredric "Fritz" Steinkamp and his son, Bill. With their colleagues and assistants, they had been working all through the shoot, receiving the dailies which were sent out each day from New York, piecing the scenes together. Sydney and Dustin had viewed

97

their assembly in New York, and when Sydney joined them, it served as the base from which he started to work.

The cutting room was on the Columbia lot in Burbank. It contained four cubicles, each big enough for a couple of people and a couple of editing machines, and it was very neat and clean and quiet. About a hundred yards away across the lot on a second floor balcony was Sydney Pollack's comfortable office, a few doors down from Dick Richards' office. The lot and all its low slung buildings toasted in the sun, assuming the color of manilla envelopes. But there was no color except the film in the dark cutting room. The gritty New York greys, the mauve and blue interiors of *Tootsie*, appeared on the small screens that rose above the editing machines. Rolls of film were fitted onto spools; one set of spools for the picture; another set for the sound. In each cubicle, the film whizzed across the tiny sprockets and through the white-gloved hands of the editors.

The various takes and accumulated dailies of *Tootsie* were stored, catalogued and organized in tight white cardboard boxes that stood by the dozen on the cutting room shelves. The scenes of the picture were listed on a lengthy continuity sheet that hung on a free wall. Each scene was described by the line or single salient message that made it most memorable. For example: Michael Dorsey in Dorothy's slip and wig stands before a closet full of clothes. He shuffles them briskly, like a customer at Bloomingdale's, saying no, this won't do; that won't do. When Jeff makes fun of him, he answers: "But it's our first date! And I want to look pretty for her!"

On the Steinkamps' wall, this scene was called: "Scene 70. Int.(erior) Loft. Michael and Jeff. Nothing to Wear.

Renee Bodner's detailed script log was of Biblical importance to the editors. Her log said how many takes were printed, which takes they were and why they were chosen. If they were no good, the log said why—maybe the sound was off or the film was blurred or the actor muffed the lines beyond repair. The log contained a kind of bank record of everything that was available that *wasn't* printed, just in case it was needed. The director's comments were preserved too, as a safeguard. If Sydney said: "That's a great first half on that take but a bad second half," Renee would record his opinion so that Fritz and Bill would know not to edit the second half of the take into the movie.

Sydney sat in the largest cubicle. On three sides of him there were Kem editing machines, each with two screens and a complex path of spools through which the sound and the picture wove. He was a changed man. His curly hair needed combing. His shirt needed ironing. He chewed on a pencil. He sped among the machines in his pliant chair, which tipped and whipped and wheeled wherever he wanted it to go, no arguments. The film was the Colorado and Sydney was God. He could make it flow, turn, twist, stop, rise, playing the electronic buttons just as he had played the keyboard during the "Famous Fashion Shoot." The editors sat behind him, and stayed as close to the door as they could because Sydney, in his racing chair, needed all the room he could get for gangway space. Every time he saw a possible cut he marked the film with a greased pencil; he said what he wanted to his editors; they noted it down; and they did it.

On the screens of one machine, there might be a master shot. On another, some close-ups. On another, the takes that Fritz and Bill didn't pick when they put together their preliminary assembly. Sydney swiveled in his chair. "What do you think?" he asked Fritz. Sometimes he didn't swivel. Sometimes he just leaned so far back that he could talk to Fritz upside down.

Because of the oncoming deadline dates, they were badly pressed for time. They chopped out pauses before lines. They chopped out beats to adjust the comic rhythm. They juggled chunks of the opening montage on Dustin as Michael Dorsey, struggling actor, with the percussionary help of some music by The New Chautauqua that Sydney had taped at home the previous night. By accident, they found a clean, clear ·cut in the acting class segment that made them all happy .

The acting class kids are listening to Michael. They hear another voice behind them. They turn. Cut. Michael is now Barney Greenwald, and he is auditioning for *The Caine Mutiny Court Martial*. "Oh that's good, that's fine," Sydney murmured happily.

On one occasion when all the editors were elsewhere, he trimmed a chunk of *Tootsie* himself, pulling the sound tape and the picture tape in a great swathe together, measuring them by eye and slicing them boldly on the razor edge of the splicer. By some miracle, the chunk came out "right on the money." However, the next time

Sydney made a cut, he threaded the tapes through all the right tension spools the way he was supposed to, and fitted them onto the sprockets and lined them up so that he could cut them with precision, and he sliced his finger and bled all over the Kem machine. "Trouble with this is your eyes go," he said sheepishly. "Editing is for young people who can see all the little holes." The editing staff gave him one of their gaily multi-colored bandaids.

Fritz Steinkamp observed these encounters between Sydney and the cut with determined mildness and a ready chuckle. A gracious, introspective man with snow white hair and moustache, he wore shorts and white socks with his sandals, looking kind of like Santa Claus would look if he were a kibbutznik. He and his Burbank staff had been working on *Tootsie* under great pressure throughout the shoot.

"The film Sydney shot on Monday in New York would be seen as dailies in New York on Tuesday," he explained. "The office would ship them to Los Angeles on Wednesday. And we would get them here in the cutting room on Thursday. So that's four days after finishing shooting. But then, there were times when Sydney couldn't run the dailies the very next night . . . so with some of them, it would be ten days before we got a complete sequence to start working on. And then with the pressure of the time element, we'd have to jam . . . awful pressure . . . time pressure . . ."

It was the second week in September. Shooting in New York had been completed the week before. By the third week in October, Sydney would have to show *Tootsie* to exhibitors from 26 non-blind bidding states. Five weeks to cut a movie that Fritz said should have been a minimum of 5–6 months in the editing. And there was so much to choose from! "Sydney prints a lot of takes," Fritz commented. "Dustin does it all kinds of different ways. And it's all good film. Hard to choose."

Now, with Sydney back home in California they worked around the clock, sculpting, pacing, honing, taking the "ums" and "uhs" and stutters out of line readings; mating "the line he got good" in one take with "the line he got good" in another take. They created energy when Jessica's was low. They created timing when Teri's was off. They created PG when Hoffman and Murray were doing R.

"It's a question of being on the right person at the right time," Sydney said. "Creating moments when there aren't any; stopping the scene; doing a double cut so that a moment that wanted a reaction now has a reaction; pacing. Not always taking the pace that was there on the take. Cutting down to the bone. Every scene doesn't have to begin at the beginning. Only when the lovers meet for the first time do you have to see every moment. Audiences are going through a real weird experience in most movies. They're dutifully eating the mashed potatoes to get to the chocolate cake. And you have to sometimes try to minimize the mashed potatoes. Of course if you *just* give them chocolate cake, that's no good either. . . . I've got too much mashed potatoes in this movie."

Sydney in his new cautionless mood accidentally trimmed *two consonants* off a word Dustin said, imperiling a very funny bit. Dustin as Dorothy is in the women's dressing room at the soap opera, cueing a fellow actress on her lines. Because she is in extremely revealing underwear, he says "tits" when he should say "tips" and immediately corrects himself. "Uh . . . *tips!*" he says emphatically. Only Sydney's trim made it play "ti . . ." One of Steinkamp's people spliced back the crucial "ps," and the laugh.

Unwanted pauses were trimmed out of the film. Julie invites Dorothy to dinner in the halls of National Video. Dorothy says "Well . . ." They took out all the space after "Well . . ." so it "wouldn't just hang there and look like acting," Sydney said, and cut immediately to Dorothy's closet and the "Nothing to Wear" episode.

To get a simple, straightforward, old-fashioned laugh in the "Baby Sitting Scene," they cut straight from Dorothy saying "How much trouble can a baby be?" to little Amy's prolonged and piercing scream.

To anchor what would be a big, screaming laugh in the "Big Reveal Scene," they took an "Oh, oh" that Dabney Coleman as Ron had said elsewhere and spliced it into the opening of Dorothy Michaels' improvised monologue on the staircase.

They came to Dorothy crossing a crowded street in New York, a long shot, and let the movie just roll. Sydney clapped his hands steadily, counting up the bars of music that Dave Grusin would have time to put in there. The more they worked, the more it appeared that editors needed to mentally *hear* the film as much as they needed to see it.

They trimmed the tips of Jessica's tipsy scenes so she would seem tipsier. They took the toasts at the surprise party off camera and made them voiceovers, so that instead of seeing the toasts and then the party, we heard the toasts and saw the party at the same time. That saved half a minute. They cut the scene in which Sandy discovers padded panty hose at Michael's apartment. Another minute saved. Bits and pieces, here and there. The first fifteen minutes came out of *Tootsie* with relative ease. The final fifteen minutes of expendable film were hardest to find because they were hardest to part with.

Dustin arrived in Burbank during the first week of the cut to view a revised assembly of the film, and to push his ideas and feelings into the editing process. "You don't become an actor because you want to do what somebody else says!" he had said. "You become an actor because you want to do it your way!" Other actors in *Tootsie* were already starting on other movies. But Dustin, who had—in Sydney's words—"fathered it along"—now stuck to it as tightly as the splicing tape, and held on, relentless in his devotion.

Suddenly in the cutting room, it became blindingly clear why the gifted writers had been as replaceable as batteries; why an impulse could make an actor look brilliant and brilliant acting could turn out to be a wasted glory. Everything that *Tootsie* might have lacked in foresight could now be made up for by hindsight. This was why Dustin Hoffman's wars were always about final cut, and why Sydney Pollack would not have directed *Tootsie* without it.

As the editing progressed, Sydney fretted about how to handle the "non-blind bidding" exhibitors. Twenty-six states had passed laws requiring film studios to show some semblance of the film that was for rent to those who would exhibit it, so that they could choose the films they wanted and bid for them on the basis of something more than "blind" faith. Should these potential customers be brought to California to see the rough cut? Or should the movie be sent around to them like a touring exhibit? "They need time to clear space," Sydney explained. "So that means a Christmas picture has to be viewed by them long before Christmas. That's what's killing me. And they're not used to seeing assemblies either, they're not used to seeing a picture without the music in it, without the dissolves, without the titles."

On the other hand, he didn't want to encourage the exhibitors to think they were seeing a finished film, if they weren't, because then they would conclude that it was less than wonderful.

"I think it's better to leave some sloppiness in it," Sydney reasoned, "because if they get the idea that they are watching the approximation of a finished picture, they're going to expect more than if they *understand* this is a rough print. . . . So it's important not to have dissolves and opticals and titles. . . . I don't even want the Columbia logo on it. 'Cause you see the Columbia logo and the torch lady and you think it's a real movie."

Ordinarily, to show the movie to exhibitors, Columbia would have hired theatres and filled them with audiences. However, since Sydney was so hard-pressed to make the Christmas dates, he finally agreed that Columbia could put the work print on videotape and send it around the country with salesmen.

Music became an increasingly vital consideration as the cut progressed. The first time Michael-as-Dorothy meets Les, he's outside the soap studio on 42nd Street and Julie turns and says "I want you to meet my father." There were other lines in the scene, less important as exposition, and Sydney didn't mind if music covered them. But then there was the traffic, the noise of the open street to contend with. He decided to loop (to record and *then* insert) Jessica's introduction "because if we need to bleed some of those lines through a song, I'd like to be able to do it real clean, without all the crap and traffic that's in it and the low frequency problems you get."

The sound of *Tootsie* and the type of song she needed were questions that Dave Grusin and Sydney considered intermittently all through the shoot. "You could have a song about honesty," Grusin suggested. "About friendship; falling in love; about being your own person. . . ." They had contacted many famous singer-composers, among them Christopher Cross and Stevie Nicks, formerly of Fleetwood Mac, but the songs-on-spec that Sydney had hoped for hadn't materialized, and time was running short. Besides, record company contracts so complicated the commitments of these performers that it was virtually impossible to have them record a song for the movie that would not interfere with the timing of their own album releases. Sydney asked his close friends, Marilyn and Alan Bergman, to write the lyrics for two songs for which Grusin composed the music. Entitled *Tootsie* and *It Might Be You,* they were sung by Stephen Bishop on the final soundtrack.

One day in the cutting room, Sydney and Fritz came to the scene in which Michael and Jeff take their long dark walk home before the surprise party. It had been a difficult night the night they shot that scene, and memories of it hung over the editing machine. Sydney stared at the frozen picture of Michael and Jeff.

Michael was depressed that night. It was his birthday. He was still waiting tables. Still a struggling actor. An aging bachelor in poverty. So Dustin was depressed too. He and Bill Murray walked up to the corner of 18th Street. Burly crewmen followed them, hauling yards of cables that slithered on the wet pavement. Behind the cables came a cluster of sound and light personnel on a silent heavy dolly, and a young Steadycam operator with the camera strapped onto his torso. Sydney yelled "Action!" The camera, the dolly, the cables went into reverse, backing down the street as Dustin and Bill walked along. With so much hardware in their faces, it was easy to see why the actors were having trouble with the lines and the emotional build of the scene. Again and again and again, the crewmen lugged the cables and pushed the dolly up to the corner, and the camera operator reset his aching back for what was becoming a longer and longer haul.

A crowd of onlookers had gathered over on the other side of the street. It was too dark to see their faces. They called Dustin's name. They demanded his attention. They weren't kidding around. He was trying to get it right, and they were pushing at him, pushing, slipping past the Production Assistants and pushing insistently.

"Please not now, honey," Dustin snapped. "I'm trying to work here."

One gaunt young man sneaked around Joe Reidy and Tom Burns. He was carrying a shopping bag. He wanted Dustin Hoffman's autograph. He reached into the shopping bag. It was a moment of terror. Hinckley time. Chapman time.

Tom Burns towered over the gaunt young man and said, "No sir, you must go back. You may not see Mr. Hoffman now. Go back there. Go."

The answering hatred on that young man's face was like a curse.

Sydney rubbed his tired eyes in Burbank and flicked the buttons so that Dustin and Bill moved along the street once more. Extras playing night people huddled in doorways. Something Bill said wasn't clear. Sydney backed up the film and ran it again. He couldn't hear it. He backed up the film and ran it again. Fritz couldn't hear it either. Sydney froze the scene and rolled to another machine to view another take. He stopped it. He pondered it.

Joe Reidy that night begged the police to please close off the street with a car, not just a little wooden horse, so that no thoughtless New York vehicle would turn into the street and bust the shoot apart. They argued. A police car was hard to give up on a dangerous night in the Big Apple. Joe argued and cajoled, and the police said no, but Joe kept trying. A thoughtless New York vehicle came around the corner, overturned the little wooden horse and frightened everyone before it stopped, shocked to find that *Tootsie* was in its path. Joe tore down the street, his headset shaking. No trouble. Nothing broken. Just scary.

The police relented. But they weren't happy. They hung out on the street, surly and annoyed.

David McGiffert tried to convince the crowd that flash pictures would destroy the carefully controlled and masked lighting of the scene. He tried to make them understand that if they stood too close or in the wrong place, their reflections would bounce back in parked cars, and ruin the shot.

But this particular crowd thought hell, this is my city, I can stand where I like, I'm not going to do what anybody tells me to do just because the street is closed off for some Hollywood movie. They stood too close. The production assistants moved them. Their cameras flashed. The production assistants argued with them. Some screeching young girls clambered out of a small theatre nearby. They laughed and hooted when they saw the scene before them. Under the pink-gelled street light, their lipstick was scarlet.

"I don't feel any support here!" Bill Murray barked at the crowd like a camp director. Some of the crew applauded. "Go, Bill!" He turned back to his fellow workers, who were dragging the shiny black python cables back to the corner for another take. "They're with us now, Sydney!" he yelled.

But they weren't. Not that night. And Dustin, who could smell the mood of strangers, knew it. "How does one not be depressed?"

he said in the shadowy doorway. It was a line in the script but he meant it with all his heart. What Sydney had said about romance in the '50s was true of 18th Street that night; something "minimally hostile" had seeped into this assignation between the major motion picture and its public. For Dustin, who was portraying an actor at the bottom of his life, the lack of love in Michael's world, the lack of love from the people in the street, was almost disabling, and they didn't get a picture they could print until the seventh take.

Bill started whistling a happy tune from an old Broadway musical. Dustin joined in. You can't sing that in the movie, Sydney cautioned, it'll cost fifteen thousand, it belongs to Disney or somebody, who does it belong to? It belonged to Gertrude Lawrence, to *The King and I*, someone said, and of course, Sydney was right, they couldn't use it. But it was a little night music and it brought the fun back and lifted the heart again and they got through the scene.

In Burbank, Sydney froze Bill and Dustin on all six screens. He toyed with the idea of looping the whole conversation in the street. Fritz Steinkamp thought that was a terrible idea. But he knew Sydney Pollack well enough to wait and say nothing until the idea gave itself up voluntarily.

"For me, every picture is a disaster," Sydney said, "a hopeless disaster until a certain point in the editing. And then it's like a light goes on inside. You don't see it the first time. You don't see it the second time. But the third time, you begin to see all the broken bones, you begin pressing on the wounds and the weak spots give way, and your fingers start going through in more and more places and you say to yourself, why did I ever get into this?! How am I gonna do a love story where she can't know he's a man until the last scene in the movie? How will I like him and still make him a chauvinist in the beginning so he has somewhere to grow toward . . . how can I make it *true* when he says he's learned to be a better man? *None of this works!* And you pull your hair out! Hours and hours of boring work, go frontwards, backwards, no, no, no, that moment's not good enough, take this out, put this in, it doesn't work, it doesn't work, it's boring boring the scene's boring, it's

SLOW! This is fun?! *This is not fun!* You go home to your kids and they say: 'How's the picture, Dad?' And you say: 'Awful awful.' 'Hahahaha, you say that all the time, Dad.' 'Yeah? Well this time I mean it.' And Claire rolls her eyes and says: 'Christ, Sydney, I've been hearing this for twenty years!' But you mean it! You mean it!

"And then some time at the third running, the fourth running, it starts to be a movie.

"It isn't finished. The color isn't right. You have to imagine the music: imagine the main titles. But the junk is on the floor, and what's there has been honed through and organized, so it starts to make some sense. And you can say: (he whispers this) *'There's a movie.'*"

He laughed. He revised his excesses, as usual. "Now of course, sometimes you're wrong," he said. "At some point, I loved *Bobby Deerfield*, which was a colossal flop."

Long ago, last week, when he was still shooting *Tootsie*, Sydney had explained that the "freebies" really served as "moments of relaxation." Dustin got his freebies, and so did all the actors on his team, and often, with an actor as true and passionate as Dustin, the freebies made it into the movie. But the director himself got no "moments of relaxation" until much later in the game. He would go into previews with "a physical fear," he said, "a fantasy that they'll turn around and say there he is, the one in the fourth row, he's the one who made this piece of shit, kill that son of a bitch!" Sydney would only get his moment of relaxation when there was nothing more to control . . . not the dizzying financial stakes; not the inquiring, exposing press; not the actors or the technology or the script . . . when time itself took everything out of his hands finally and *Tootsie* became historical; a fact; a bit of the record; *an old movie.* "I think if you do twenty pictures in your life," he said, "five of them will be terrific, and five of them will be just horrible, and ten will be okay. And they'll pick out in 1999 what they want to pick out and they'll make me a bum or they'll forget me or they'll make Marty Scorsese a bum or a genius or whatever or Ridley Scott or George Roy Hill or whoever and *the biggest mistake any of us can make is to say, well, I'm gonna wait until this great piece of art comes along and then I'm gonna work.*"

Somebody called Sydney Pollack in the cutting room, and asked how it was going. "Oh it's hard," he said distractedly. "It's hard it's hard it's fine it's fu . . ." He laughed, self-consciously, because he had almost said "It's fun."

Tootsie opened nationally December 17, 1982 in over 900 theatres. By January 17, 1983 the picture was playing in 1190 theatres in the United States and Canada. It had grossed $69,277,522, more than twice the amount of its nearest competition among the Christmas releases which included *The Toy, 48 Hours, Dark Crystal, Best Friends,* and *The Verdict* in their box office ranking order after *Tootsie.*

The National Society of Film Critics had named it best picture of the year; Dustin Hoffman best actor, Jessica Lange best supporting actress, and cited its script as best screenplay. The New York Film Critics named Sydney Pollack best director of the year and also singled out Lange for her supporting role and Gelbart and Schisgal for the screenplay. *Tootsie,* Hoffman, Pollack, Lange, Gelbart and Schisgal had all received Golden Globe nominations.

Marvin Antonowsky, head of marketing at Columbia, predicted that *Tootsie'*s eventual grosses would exceed the $140 million Columbia record set by *Close Encounters of the Third Kind.* This would put *Tootsie* in a financial league with *The Godfather* and *The Sound of Music,* placing it among the top twelve film rental earners of all time and making it the most successful Columbia Pictures film, ever.

FILMS STARRING DUSTIN HOFFMAN

Year of Release	Feature	Directed by
1967	The Tiger Makes Out	Arthur Hiller
1967	The Graduate	Mike Nichols
1968	Madigan's Millions	Stanley Prager
1969	John and Mary	Peter Yates
1969	Midnight Cowboy	John Schlesinger
1970	Little Big Man	Arthur Penn
1971	Who Is Harry Kellerman and Why Is He Saying Those Terrible Things About Me?	Ulu Grosbard
1971	Straw Dogs	Sam Peckinpah
1972	Alfredo Alfredo	Pietro Germi
1973	Papillon	Franklin Schaffner
1974	Lenny	Bob Fosse
1976	All the President's Men	Alan J. Pakula
1976	Marathon Man	John Schlesinger
1978	Straight Time	Ulu Grosbard
1979	Agatha	Michael Apted
1979	Kramer Vs. Kramer	Robert Benton
1982	Tootsie	Sydney Pollack

FILMS DIRECTED BY SYDNEY POLLACK

Year of Release	Feature	Cast Included
1965	The Slender Thread	Sidney Poitier, Anne Bancroft, Telly Savalas
1966	This Property is Condemned	Natalie Wood, Robert Redford, Charles Bronson
1968	The Swimmer (directed one sequence only in a film of Frank Perry)	Burt Lancaster, Janice Rule, Kim Hunter
1968	The Scalphunters	Burt Lancaster, Ossie Davis, Shelley Winters, Telly Savalas
1969	Castle Keep	Burt Lancaster, Peter Falk, Patrick O'Neal
1969/70	They Shoot Horses, Don't They?	Jane Fonda, Michael Sarrazin, Gig Young
1972	Jeremiah Johnson (also producer)	Robert Redford, Will Geer
1973	The Way We Were	Barbra Streisand, Robert Redford
1975	The Yakuza (also producer)	Robert Mitchum, Brian Keith
1975	Three Days of the Condor	Robert Redford, Faye Dunaway, Cliff Robertson, Max von Sydow, John Houseman
1977	Bobby Deerfield (also producer)	Al Pacino, Marthe Keller
1979	The Electric Horseman	Robert Redford, Jane Fonda
1981	Absence of Malice (also producer)	Paul Newman, Sally Field
1982	Tootsie (also producer)	Dustin Hoffman, Jessica Lange, Teri Garr

Greg Gorman

Tootsie

CREDITS

COLUMBIA PICTURES PRESENTS
A SYDNEY POLLACK FILM
A MIRAGE/PUNCH PRODUCTION

THE CAST

Michael Dorsey/Dorothy Michaels	DUSTIN HOFFMAN
Julie	JESSICA LANGE
Sandy	TERI GARR
Ron	DABNEY COLEMAN
Les	CHARLES DURNING
Jeff	BILL MURRAY
George Fields	SYDNEY POLLACK
John Van Horn	GEORGE GAYNES
April	GEENA DAVIS
Rita	DORIS BELACK
Jacqui	ELLEN FOLEY
Rick	PETER GATTO
Jo	LYNNE THIGPEN
Phil Weintraub	RONALD L. SCHWARY
Mrs. Mallory	DEBRA MOONEY
Amy	AMY LAWRENCE
Boy	KENNY SINCLAIR
Page	SUSAN MERSON
Middle-Aged Man	MICHAEL RYAN
Stage Hand	ROBERT D. WILSON
Middle-Aged Man	JAMES CARRUTHERS
Middle-Aged Woman	ESTELLE GETTY

Linda	CHRISTINE EBERSOLE
Actor #1	BERNIE POLLACK
Actor #2	SAM STONEBURNER
Salesgirl	MARJORIE LOVETT
Man at Cab	WILLY SWITKES
Maitre d'	GREGORY CAMILLUCCI
Billie	BARBARA SPIEGEL
Joel Spector	TONY CRAIG
Bartender	WALTER CLINE
Party Girl	SUZANNE VON SCHAACK
Mrs. Crawley	ANNE SHROPSHIRE
Secretary	PAMELA LINCOLN
Receptionist	MARY DONNET
Mac	BERNIE PASSELTINER
Girl #1	MALLORY JONES
Girl #2	PATTI COHANE
Party Guest	MURRAY SCHISGAL
Photographer	GREG GORMAN
Acting Student	ANNE PRAGER
First Actor	JOHN CARPENTER
Second Actor	BOB LEVINE
Priest	RICHARD WHITING
Stage Manager #2	JIM JANSEN
Diane	SUSAN EGBERT
Acting Student	KAS SELF
Stage Manager	TOM MARDIROSIAN
Mel (Technical Director)	RICHARD WIRTH
Director	GAVIN REED
Autograph Hounds	ANNIE KORZEN, IBBITS WARRINER, LOIS DE BANZIE, STEPHEN C. PRUTTING, CAROLE HOLLAND

THE PRODUCTION TEAM

Director	SYDNEY POLLACK
Producers	SYDNEY POLLACK and DICK RICHARDS
Story by	DON McGUIRE and LARRY GELBART
Screenplay by	LARRY GELBART and MURRAY SCHISGAL
Director of Photography	OWEN ROIZMAN, A.S.C.

114

Production Designed by .... PETER LARKIN
Executive Producer .... CHARLES EVANS
Edited by .... FREDRIC STEINKAMP and WILLIAM STEINKAMP
Music .... DAVE GRUSIN
Costumes Designed by .... RUTH MORLEY
Casting .... LYNN STALMASTER, TONI HOWARD & ASSOCIATES
Unit Production Manager .... GERALD R. MOLEN
Assistant Director .... DAVID McGIFFERT
Second Assistant Director .... JOSEPH REIDY
Mr. Hoffman's Make-Up Created and Designed by .... DOROTHY PEARL,
                                                        GEORGE MASTERS
Costume Supervisor .... BERNIE POLLACK
Auditor .... KEN RYAN
Men's Costumer .... FRANKE PIAZZA
Women's Costumer .... JENNIFER NICHOLS
Make-Up Artist .... C. ROMANIA FORD
Mr. Hoffman's Make-Up .... ALLEN WEISINGER
Hair Stylists .... JOE COSCIA, TONY MARRERO
Ms. Lange's Make-Up .... DOROTHY PEARL
Ms. Lange's Hair Stylist .... TONI WALKER
Set Decorator .... TOM TONERY
Camera Operator .... BILL STEINER
Camera First Assistant .... MICHAEL GREEN
Camera Second Assistant .... SCOTT RATHNER
Unit Publicist .... ANN GUERIN
Sound Mixer .... LES LAZAROWITZ
Boom Man .... TOD MAITLAND, M.P.E.
Gaffer .... DICK QUINLAN
Key Grips .... BOB ROSE, MICHAEL MILLER
Property Master .... JIMMY RAITT
Extras Casting .... SYLVIA FAY
Assistant Editors .... NANCY WEIZER, DON BROCHU
Music Editor .... ELSE BLANGSTED
Assistant Auditor .... PETE LOMBARDI
Transportation Captain .... WHITEY McEVOY
Sound Effects .... EFFECTIVE SOUND UNLIMITED,
                                    TOM McCARTHY JR., DON WALDEN
Re-Recording Mixers .... ARTHUR PIANTADOSI, C.A.S.,
                                            LES FRESHOLTZ, C.A.S.,
                                          DICK ALEXANDER, C.A.S.
Location Managers .... ERZA SWERDLOW, JONATHAN FILLEY
DGA Trainee .... ANN EGBERT
Production Office Coordinator .... BRUCE PATTERSON
Assistant Production Office Coordinator .... HARRIETTE KANEW
Assistant to Dustin Hoffman .... LEE GOTTSEGEN
Assistant to Sydney Pollack .... CRIN CONNOLLY

115

Unit Still Photographer .... BRIAN HAMILL
Script Supervisor .... RENEE BODNER
Production Assistants .... TOM BURNS, JUSTIN COOKE, SALLY BRIM,
CAREY BOZANICH, STEPHANIE BROOKS,
GARY VERMILLION, KARL STEINKAMP, TONY LANI

Original Songs
Lyrics by ALAN & MARILYN BERGMAN
Music by DAVE GRUSIN

"Tootsie"
"It Might Be You"
Sung by STEPHEN BISHOP

INDEX

Absence of Malice, 3, 26, 49, 83
Academy Awards, 2
Adler, Stella, 11, 95
Alfredo, Alfredo, 30, 53
Allen, Woody, 16
All That Jazz, 15
All the President's Men, 2
American Film (magazine), 49, 84
Annie Hall, 28
Ann-Margret, 4
Anspach, Susan, 79
Antonowsky, Marvin, 108
Arkin, Alan, 37
Ashby, Hal, 9–10

Baker's Dozen, 14
Baryshnikov, Mikhail, 6
Beckett, Samuel, 77, 79
Belack, Doris, 14
Ben Casey, 48
Benmussa, Simone, 2
Bergman, Alan, 103
Bergman, Marilyn, 103
Best Friends, 17, 108
Bishop, Billy, 39
Bishop, Stephen, 104
Black Stallion, The, 57
Black Sunday, 8
Bobby Deerfield, 3, 52, 107
Bodner, Renee, 79, 98
Bound for Glory, 9
Brando, Marlon, 62
Brooks, Mel, 16
Brown, Joe E., 1

Burns, George, 26
Burns, Tom, 64, 104
Burstyn, Ellen, 61

Caddyshack, 78
Caesar's Hour, 16
Cage Aux Folles I, La, 1
Cage Aux Folles II, La, 1
Caine Mutiny Court Martial, The, 99
Candid Camera, 47
Castellano, Richard, 79
Chase, Chevy, 8
Chrysler Theatre, 48
Churchill, Caryl, 2
Clark, Brian, 13
Close, Glenn, 2
Close Encounters of the Third Kind, 57, 108
Cloud 9, 2
Clurman, Harold, 11, 12
Cohn, Sam, 90, 91
Coleman, Dabney, 15, 34, 76, 101
Coming Home, 10
Cooke, Justin, 64
Coppola, Francis Ford, 89
Coscia, Joe, 93
Creative Artists Agency, 64
Cross, Christopher, 103
Curtin, Valerie, 17
Curtis, Tony, 1

Dancin', 26
Dark Crystal, 108
Dean, Jimmy, 62

Death of a Salesman, 36
Defenders, The, 48
De Niro, Robert, 29
Derek, Bo, 24
Donnet, Mary, 65
Dunaway, Fay, 3
Durning, Charles, 5, 13
Duvall, Robert, 62, 79

Eastwood, Clint, 84
Egbert, Ann, 19, 20
Eh, 37, 68
Electric Horseman, The, 3, 17, 71, 87
Endgame, 77
Esquire (magazine), 49
Evans, Bob, 8, 33
Evans, Charles, 7, 8, 9

Farnum, Dustin, 62
Father, The, 95
Fay, Sylvia, 32
Field, Sally, 3
Fields, Lew, 71–72
Figaro, Le (paper), 64, 83
Fonda, Jane, 3, 49
Ford, Rumania, 77
48 Hours, 108
Fosse, Bob, 91
Frances, 15
Frankenheimer, John, 48
Funny Thing Happened on the Way to the Forum, A, 16

Game, The, 49
Garland, Robert, 17
Garr, Teri, 5, 13, 53, 56–57, 89–94, 100
Gaynor, George, 13–14, 34
Gelbart, Larry, 4, 10, 16–17, 79, 108
Godfather, The, 108
Golden Globe, 108
Goldoni, Carlo, 16
Gorman, Greg, 39
Gottschalk, Bobo, 26
Gould, Elliott, 8
Graduate, The, 2, 13, 36, 63
Greenwald, Barney, 99

Grosbard, Ulu, 79
Grusin, Dave, 103
Guerin, Ann, 64

Hackett, Buddy, 7, 15
Hackman, Gene, 62, 63
Hamill, Brian, 39
Hamilton, George, 8
Hill, George Roy, 107
Hoffman, Dustin, 1, 3–4, 5–6, 7–8, 9, 10–23, 28–29, 33–47, 51–55, 57, 61–66, 68–70, 79–80, 82, 88–89, 93, 97, 99–100, 102, 104–8
Hoffman, Lillian, 62
Hoffman, Lisa, 82, 97
Hoffman, Ronald, 62
Holliday, Polly, 14
Howe, James Wong, 49–50

Iceman Cometh, The, 5, 65, 66
Importance of Being Earnest, The, 36
Indecent Exposure, 83
International Creative Management, 90
It's My Turn, 7

Jackson, Anne, 9
Jeremiah Johnson, 3
Jimmy Shine, 9
Jonson, Ben, 16
Journey of the Fifth House, 68

Kaufman, Bob, 7, 8
Kazan, Elia, 1
King and I, The, 106
King Kong, 14, 53, 90
Kiss Me Kate, 58
Kramer vs. Kramer, 2, 28–29, 48, 71

Ladies' Home Journal, 63
Lancaster, Burt, 48
Lang, Rocky, 4, 27, 36, 49, 64
Lange, Jessica, 5, 14–15, 51, 53–55, 100, 108
Larkin, Peter, 18, 25, 53, 77
Lawrence, Gertrude, 106
Lazarowitz, Les, 23
Le Carré, John, 96

Lemmon, Jack, 1
Lenny, 2
Levinson, Barry, 17
Life (magazine), 83
Lithgow, John, 1
Little Big Man, 23
Looking To Get Out, 10
Loren, Sophia, 53
Love at First Bite, 8
Lucek, Bill, 18
Luv, 9

Maitland, Tod, 60
Manhattan Theatre Club, 2
Marathon Man, 8
Marrero, Tony, 22, 39
Mary Hartman, Mary Hartman, 15
M*A*S*H, 4, 10, 16
Maslin, Janet, 33, 83
Masters, George, 23–24, 25
May, Elaine, 17, 89
McClintock, David, 83
McGiffert, David, 6, 18, 19, 49, 58, 64, 65, 72, 76, 79, 90, 105
McGuire, Don, 7
Meatballs, 78
Meisner, Sanford, 11, 12, 62
Meryman, Dick, 63
Midnight Cowboy, 2, 82
Miller, Arthur, 79
Miracle Worker, The, 28
Monroe, Marilyn, 1, 14, 53
Morley, Ruth, 28–33, 53, 56, 77–78
Morrison, George, 62
Mostel, Zero, 16
Murray, Bill, 5, 14, 51, 78, 79, 100, 104, 105, 106

Naked City, 48, 63
National Society of Film Critics, 108
New Chautauqua, The, 99
Newman, Paul, 3
New York Film Critics, 108
New York Times, The, 83
Nichols, Jennifer, 32, 38, 39

Nichols, Mike, 36, 68
Nicks, Stevie, 103
9 To 5, 15

Odets, Clifford, 12
Officer and a Gentleman, An, 90
Oh God!, 56
One from the Heart, 89
On Golden Pond, 15
Ordinary People, 26
Ovitz, Michael, 64

Pacino, Al, 3, 51–52
Pearl, Dorothy, 25
Piazza, Franke, 39
Plautus, 16
Playboy (magazine), 63
Plitt, Henry, 7, 9, 87
Pollack, Claire, 96, 107
Pollack, Sydney, 2, 3–4, 5, 7, 8–21, 26–27, 32, 39, 40, 42–55, 65, 68, 71–80, 81–89, 93, 94–108
Postman Always Rings Twice, The, 15
Price, Frank, 85

Redford, Lola, 96
Redford, Robert, 3, 42, 49, 51, 96
Reidy, Joe, 77, 78, 104, 105
Reiner, Carl, 16
Reinhardt, Max, 95
Richards, Dick, 8, 9
Rocky, 70
Roizman, Owen, 6, 18–19, 24, 26, 32, 40, 48, 50–51, 92
Russians Are Coming, The, 37
Ryan, Michael M., 43, 48

Sansweet, Stephen, 84
Saturday Night Live, 14
Scheider, Roy, 91
Schisgal, Murray, 4, 8–9, 17, 29, 108
Schisgal, Renee, 82
Schwary, Ron, 26–27, 51, 87
Scorsese, Marty, 107
Scott, George C., 16
Scott, Ridley, 107
Scott, Zachary, 15

Segal, George, 8
Self, Kas, 39
Sergeant Musgrave's Dance, 68
Servant of Two Masters, 16
Simon, Neil, 16
Singular Life of Albert Nobbs, The, 2
Siskel, Gene, 37
Shahn, Ben, 79
Shakespeare, William, 16
Shelby, David, 23
Shevelove, Burt, 16
Show of Shows, The, 16
Slender Thread, The, 49
Sly Fox, 16
Smith, Dick, 23, 25
Some Like It Hot, 1
Sound of Music, The, 108
Southwest General, 38
Springer, John, 82
Stalmaster, Lynn, 13
Stanislavsky, Konstantin, 12
Steinkamp, Bill, 97, 98
Steinkamp, Fredric (Fritz), 97, 98,
   99, 100, 104–5, 106
Straight Time, 9, 10, 30, 62
Strasberg, Lee, 11, 12, 95
Straw Dogs, 2
Streep, Meryl, 91
Streetcar Named Desire, A, 36
Streisand, Barbra, 1, 3, 49
Stripes, 78
Swerdlow, Ezra, 82

Taxi Driver, 29
Taylor, Elizabeth, 53
Teahouse of the August Moon, 25
They Shoot Horses, Don't They?, 3, 49
This Property Is Condemned, 3, 49

Three Days of the Condor, 3, 42, 50
Tonight Show, The, 91
Toy, The, 108
Tune, Tommy, 2
Twelfth Night, 16, 17
Twice Around the Park, 9
Typist and the Tiger, The, 9

Variety (paper), 11, 84, 87
Verdict, The, 108
Victor, Victoria, 1
View From the Bridge, A, 79, 82
Voight, Jon, 10, 79, 82
Volpone, 16

Waiting for Godot, 77
Waiting for Lefty, 12
Wallach, Eli, 9
Waltzer, Jack, 70
War Hunt, The, 49
Way We Were, The, 3, 13, 49, 88
Weber, Joe, 71–72
Weisinger, Allen, 23, 24, 25, 27, 40
Welch, Raquel, 53
West Side Story, 91
Whose Life Is It Anyway?, 13
Wilder, Billy, 1
Wilson, Bobby, 35
Wittich, Kato, 64, 65
World According To Garp, The, 1
Would I Lie To You?, 7–8

Yakuza, The, 50
Yentl, 1
Young Frankenstein, 13, 57
Young Savages, The, 48

Zorro, The Gay Blade, 8

ABOUT THE AUTHOR

SUSAN DWORKIN's most recent work before *Making Tootsie* was *She's Nobody's Baby*, a one-hour documentary film about American women in the 20th century. Produced by the Ms. Foundation for Education and Communication, starring Marlo Thomas and Alan Alda, the film premiered on Home Box Office and won the coveted Peabody Award for excellence in broadcasting.

With Dr. Cynthia W. Cooke, she wrote *The Ms. Guide to a Woman's Health* which received an American Book Award nomination. As a contributing editor at *Ms.* Magazine and a frequent contributor to other national publications, she has interviewed many people in show business including Stella Adler, Meryl Streep, Jane Alexander, Gloria Foster, Lola Redford and Marlo Thomas. She has worked closely with Ms. Thomas for several years, both on television projects and the McCall Life Pattern Fund to support continuing education for women. She has also worked as head of the Writing Unit of the Office of Policy Research at New York's Department of Social Services and as a speech writer for the Commissioner of Welfare.

Ms. Dworkin's work in the theater has received considerable attention. The *New York Times* called her play, *Deli's Fable*, "an authentic work of the imagination . . . a triumph." Other plays produced in New York include: *The Ghost Convention, The Public Good*, and most recently *The Forgotten Lover*. Ms. Dworkin was the founder and director of Bergenstage, a professional theater in northern New Jersey where she lives.